# 10

## THINGS
## YOU
## CAN DO!

# ACTION FOR DISARMAMENT

# 10 THINGS YOU CAN DO!

**UNITED NATIONS**

Unexploded ordnance being prepared for destruction by explosive disposal technicians in a remote desert area of Libya.

# TABLE OF CONTENTS

*Action for Disarmament: 10 Things You Can Do*

Published by the United Nations Department of Public Information in cooperation with the United Nations Office for Disarmament Affairs
New York, New York 10017

All queries on rights and licences, including subsidiary rights, should be addressed to:
United Nations Publications, 300 East 42nd Street, New York, NY 10017, United States of America;
*e-mail:* publications@un.org; *website:* unp.un.org/

ISBN:  978-92-1-142287-0
eISBN: 978-92-1-054111-4
United Nations Publication
Sales No. E.13.IX.6

*Design:* Graphic Design Unit, Department of Public Information, United Nations, New York

Special thanks to Kathleen Sullivan and Peter Lucas who were the primary authors of this book.

We are grateful for the permission granted by the Nagasaki Atomic Bomb Museum and the Nagasaki Foundation for the Promotion of Peace to use photographs and atomic bomb survivors' artwork in this book.

I   INTRODUCTION

II   10 THINGS YOU CAN DO

III   CONCLUSION

**BEFORE**

US Army photographs of Nagasaki City
before and after the atomic bombing

AFTER

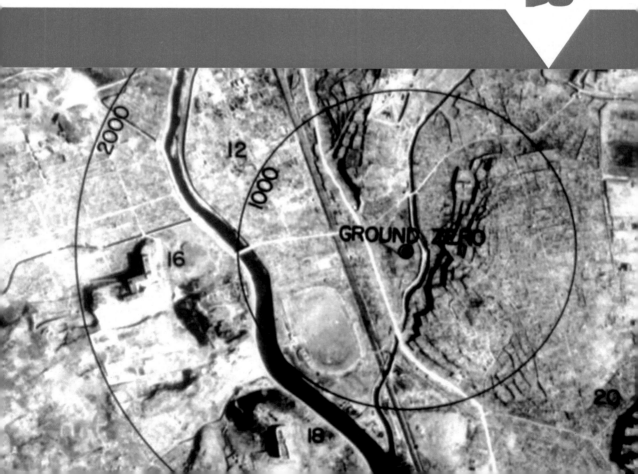

Survivor's artwork after the
atomic bombing in Nagasaki City

"We must not only control the weapons that can kill us, we must bridge the great disparities of wealth and opportunity among the peoples of the world, the vast majority of whom live in poverty without hope, opportunity or choices in life. These conditions are a breeding ground for division that can cause a desperate people to resort to nuclear weapons as a last resort. Our only hope lies in the power of our love, generosity, tolerance and understanding and our commitment to making the world a better place for all."

Muhammad Ali, ◄
former United Nations
Messenger of Peace

# FOREWORD

With 1.8 billion young people between the ages of 10 and 24 in the world today, you make up the largest generation of youth the world has ever known. Access to education, employment, human rights, the threat of climate change are but a few of the challenges you face.

The UN Secretary-General has made "working with and for young people" one of his top five priorities. In support of his youth agenda, I am working throughout the UN system to ensure that you, as young people, are included in the decision-making process on policy issues that affect your lives.

This book draws your attention to another global issue of importance—the need to promote peace and security in the world through disarmament.

One aspect of disarmament focuses on nuclear weapons. People born after the end of the Cold War have been spared growing up under the fear of a nuclear attack. Yet the risk posed by nuclear weapons still exists today. As Secretary-General Ban Ki-moon noted, "Sadly, we know the terrible humanitarian consequences from the use of even one [nuclear] weapon. As long as such weapons exist, so, too, will the risks of use and proliferation."

Another aspect of disarmament addresses the illicit trade in small arms and light weapons. Most present-day conflicts are fought with small arms and light weapons. They are the weapons of choice in civil wars, organized crime, gang warfare and terrorist attacks. They are easy to use, to carry, and to conceal. Illicit flows of small arms and light weapons undermine security and the rule of law, undermine economic and social development, and are often a factor behind the forced displacement of civilians and massive human rights violations.

Youth have a critical role to play in getting the public at large to participate in developing new strategies to reduce the threats to international peace and security posed by these weapons. The disarmament agenda cannot be ignored. The future of humanity depends upon it.

Youth have shown time and again that they are the drivers of change. We are counting on you to make your voices heard on this critical issue. To give you some important tools, we have prepared this book, *Action for Disarmament: 10 Things You Can Do*, which is filled with ideas and resources to help you make the public aware of why disarmament is important.

I look forward to working with you to make our planet safer for us, and for generations to come!

—**Ahmad Alhendawi,** *United Nations Secretary-General's Envoy on Youth*

# PREFACE

The outbreak of World War I in 1914 was a watershed for the technological advancement of modern weapons. Never before was a major war fought with weapons forged from the industrial revolution. There was the machine gun, as well as artillery capable of firing exploding shells from several miles away. Landmines were planted in the fields. There were armoured tanks, battleships, and even submarines firing torpedoes. From above, warplanes were dropping bombs. As a harbinger of things to come, mustard gas was also released as a chemical weapon. For four years, there was an average of five and a half thousand casualties per day. In the end, 10 million people died and 30 million were wounded, maimed, disfigured, and incapacitated for the rest of their lives. The world had changed: mankind had the technical means to mass-produce destruction.

World War II continued that trend—now widening the annihilation to civilian populations. This war also saw the birth of the nuclear age with the emergence of nuclear weapons. The mere existence of nuclear weapons—which can wipe out civilizations, even life on earth—has changed our world forever.

In the decades after World War II, the Cold War between the major powers sometimes led to proxy wars in other parts of the world. The two largest nuclear-weapon States, the United States and the Soviet Union, provided conventional arms to countries who then fought wars sometimes for independence and sometimes for ideological reasons, which resulted in millions of casualties.

After 1990, when the Cold War ended, the number of conflicts went down, and their character changed. Inter-State warfare (soldiers from different countries fighting each other) had been largely replaced by ethnic and religious strife, with armed groups mixing economic and political objectives, mainly using small arms and light weapons. All too often those handling guns had acquired them illegally, often from the excessively large Cold War stocks left around the world.

All in all, nowadays the world's governments are spending well over US$ 1.5 trillion a year on their militaries, a level of spending not seen since the end of World War II. This amounts to roughly $250 for each person in the world. Whereas 2.5% of the world's gross domestic product goes to the military, only 0.3%—eight times less—is spent on development aid.

People born after the Cold War have grown up without the persistent cloud of living under the threat of a global nuclear war. Instead of some 60,000 nuclear warheads that were around in 1991, there are now approximately 17,000 of them. The threat of two global powers entering a full-scale nuclear war has receded, but because of the ability of nuclear arms to obliterate whole societies—and the risk of misuse, loss, or unforeseen political developments—the problem is not in the numbers, but in the mere existence of these weapons.

Disarmament education is needed more than ever to make us grasp the present-day reality of these threats. The goal of *Action for Disarmament* is to encourage dialogue among, and provide disarmament and non-proliferation resources to, all who care about the future. It also aims to spread the message that disarmament provides a foundation for promoting peace and development around the world.

All people, especially youth, can play a valuable role by taking action to create a safer world—from nuclear weapons abolition to curbing gun violence.

Before deciding which aspect of disarmament and non-proliferation you are most interested in, it is important to know the many types of weapons that exist in the world today—to understand how they have evolved and continue to proliferate.

Weapons being burnt during the official launch of the "Disarmament, Demobilization, Rehabilitation and Reintegration" process in Burundi.

**"There can be no development without peace and no peace without development. Disarmament can provide the means for both. With your voice and strong support, we can get this message across and advance the international disarmament agenda."**

*United Nations Secretary-General Ban Ki-moon—message to the Religions for Peace Global Youth Campaign on Disarmament for Shared Security in San José, Costa Rica, November 2009*

# CATEGORIES

Radiation Warning symbol

Biohazard symbol

**NUCLEAR WEAPONS:** The most dangerous weapons in the world are nuclear weapons: a threat to all life on earth. These weapons cause a massive explosion through what is called nuclear fission: the splitting of an atom, which creates a sudden, tremendous release of energy.

The effects of a nuclear explosion include blast, heat, and radiation, producing destruction on an unimaginable scale. Immense light and thermal heat—comparable to the interior of the sun—cause what is called a firestorm, depleting oxygen from the environment and creating hurricane-like winds that attract debris and feed the storm itself, causing super-infernos. Another effect of a nuclear explosion is radiation. Once released, radioactive elements can hang around for millennia, putting future generations at risk of cancer and genetic mutations. The destructive power of nuclear weapons has been described as "unthinkable".

**BIOLOGICAL AND CHEMICAL WEAPONS:** Biological weapons have existed since antiquity: historical accounts from medieval Europe detail the use of infected animal carcasses thrown over besieged cities' walls and in wells to infect enemy combatants and civilian populations. More recently, in World War I, both sides fired projectiles that released poisonous gases such as mustard gas, which is a mix of carbon, chlorine, hydrogen, and sulfur. Biological and toxin weapons differ from chemical weapons in that biological weapons use bacteria or viruses, or in some cases toxins that come directly from bacteria, to kill people. An example is ebola, a highly contagious bacterial agent which can be disseminated through a variety of delivery systems. Chemical, biological and toxin weapons are so lethal that their development, production, stockpiling and use are prohibited through international treaties. The stockpiling of

# OF WEAPONS

these kinds of weapons poses great risks because of their potential to be deployed within a relatively short period of time.

**RADIOLOGICAL WEAPONS:** Also called radiological dispersion devises (RDDs) or "dirty bombs", radiological weapons could be used to spread economic and social disruption through the dispersal of invisible radioactive contaminants. Although they are capable of extensive, long-term damage, have the potential to be used for spreading terror and panic, RDDs have not been used in war, but the fear that they might be used has increased in recent years. Anxiety about radiological weapons has fuelled a debate about the operation of nuclear power plants. Nuclear power plants utilize and create radioactive materials in the form of spent fuel storage and other on-site radioactive waste that could be fashioned into radiological weapons. A growing concern is that these radioactive materials might be stolen and used to cause damage to people and the environment.

Some people argue that nuclear power plants themselves could be used as radiological weapons. For example, in the event of war, nuclear power plants could be used as primary bombing targets, having the potential to release widespread radioactive material. There is no agreement on the actual damage that a radiological weapon could produce because that would depend upon the type of radioactive materials used, and how they were dispersed.

**MAJOR CONVENTIONAL WEAPONS:** When we talk about weapons and war, we're usually thinking about conventional weapons systems. Think of battle tanks, armoured combat vehicles, artillery systems, attack helicopters, combat aircraft, warships, and missile systems. Each year, countries spend an enormous amount of money on these weapons; the trade in

The plutonium bomb "Fat Man" that was dropped over the City of Nagasaki on 9 August 1945, killing more than 70,000 people, and causing radiation sickness in survivors that continues to this day.

Over 75 kilos of unexploded ordnance (UXOs), captured from al-Shabaab militants, are destroyed outside of Mogadishu, Somalia, at a safe location.

heavy conventional arms is big business. But more weapons in a region can mean the prolongation and intensification of conflict. Also, the transfer of conventional arms to States that have a troubled history with democracy, human rights, and non-proliferation is a recurring problem. That is why, in 2013, the United Nations (UN) General Assembly adopted the landmark Arms Trade Treaty. It creates a level playing field for the global arms trade, bringing to it more accountability, openness and transparency, and making it harder for human rights abusers, criminals and arms traffickers to obtain weapons. All important weapons systems are covered by the treaty: battle tanks, armoured personnel carriers, artillery, fighter jets, attack helicopters warships, missiles, small arms and light weapons as well as ammunition.

> "It is a historic achievement—the culmination of long-held dreams and many years of effort. This is a victory for the world's people. The Arms Trade Treaty will make it more difficult for deadly weapons to be diverted into the illicit market, and it will help to keep warlords, pirates, terrorists, criminals and their like from acquiring deadly arms. It will be a powerful new tool in our efforts to prevent grave human rights abuses or violations of international humanitarian law."
>
> —*Secretary-General Ban Ki-moon on the adoption of the Arms Trade Treaty by the United Nations General Assembly on 2 April 2013*

**LANDMINES AND CLUSTER BOMBS:** Although categorized as conventional weapons, landmines and cluster bombs are often treated as a category in and of themselves because of their inhumane impact in post-conflict situations. These weapons are problematic because their victims are often civilians. Roughly one third are women and children. Landmines and cluster munitions remain long after the conflict has ended. Landmines are very expensive to detect and remove. They are cheap to deploy but difficult to uncover. It is estimated that there are 60 million landmines planted in the world's conflict areas.

The International Campaign to Ban Landmines estimates that landmines cause over 4,000 casualties each year—that is 11 to 12 per day. Women and children are often the victims losing their lives, limbs, or eyesight from accidentally contacting an explosive device.

Like landmines, cluster bombs are almost impossible to target only military, and they are often still set to explode long after the fighting has ended. Cluster bombs are shot with artillery or dropped from airplanes, containing sub-munitions or "bomblets", which disperse over a wide area. The colourful explosive duds have often killed and maimed children who mistake them for a toy or a ball.

United Nations "Blue Helmets" help disarm militias in Côte d'Ivoire.

**SMALL ARMS AND LIGHT WEAPONS:** Most armed violence in the world is perpetrated with small arms and light weapons, which is why they are sometimes called "the real weapons of mass destruction". Technically, "small arms" refers to firearms that can be easily carried by a single person. These include handguns, rifles, carbines, submachine guns, assault rifles, and light hand-held machine guns.

Light weapons need to be operated by two or three people. These include grenade launchers, mortars, light missiles, portable anti-tank and anti-aircraft guns, heavy machine guns, cannons, and various explosive devices. Like major conventional arms, the international trade in light weapons in principle involves government-to-government transfers—but there seems to be a large international black market for them.

Most present-day conflicts are fought mainly with small arms, which are broadly used in inter-State conflict. They are the weapons of choice in civil wars and for terrorism, organized crime and gang warfare because they are cheap, light, and easy to handle, transport and conceal.

The proliferation of small arms and light weapons can encourage conflicts, undermine peace initiatives, and exacerbate human rights abuses. Armed conflict causes people to flee their homes and is the most common cause of food insecurity. In addition, armed violence also diverts energy and resources away from efforts to improve human development. As the violence in a conflict zone becomes more lethal and lasts longer,

A section of ground is cordoned off during an exercise held by the United Nations Mine Action Service in Mogadishu, Somalia, as part of the International Day of Mine Awareness.

a sense of insecurity grows, which in turn leads to a greater demand for weapons.

Since 2001, the UN has recognized the grave threat posed by small arms and light weapons in the wrong hands. The UN Programme of Action on the illicit trade in small arms and light weapons provides a framework for activities to counter this global threat. It is not about banning small arms or prohibiting people from owning legal weapons and it does not suggest any action against the legal trade, manufacture, possession or ownership of weapons. Its sole focus is on countering the illicit trade in small arms and light weapons and preventing the diversion of weapons into black markets.

Today, disarmament is increasingly important because military spending and the proliferation of weapons have never been higher. Students can engage in exciting and empowering activities to increase awareness about disarmament and non-proliferation and also to take action based on their knowledge and analysis of the subject. This book aims to take learning beyond the classroom, providing a range of suggested activities with you, the student, in mind, so that you can find inspiration in what you have learned and be a part of making a difference.

The United Nations' shared vision for all students is this —that you help alleviate violence in the world through raising awareness and taking action. *Action for Disarmament: 10 Things You Can Do* is meant to help you become an agent for social change. Many of you may know these educational strategies, but they may be slightly different in relation to disarmament. Besides disarmament, these steps can also be used in the context of other important social and environmental issues.

Feel free to choose and select which aspects best fit your learning environment. These Ten Things are not meant to be done in any particular order. Mix and match. Be creative in choosing which strategy is best for you.

# WORLD MILITARY EXPENDITURE

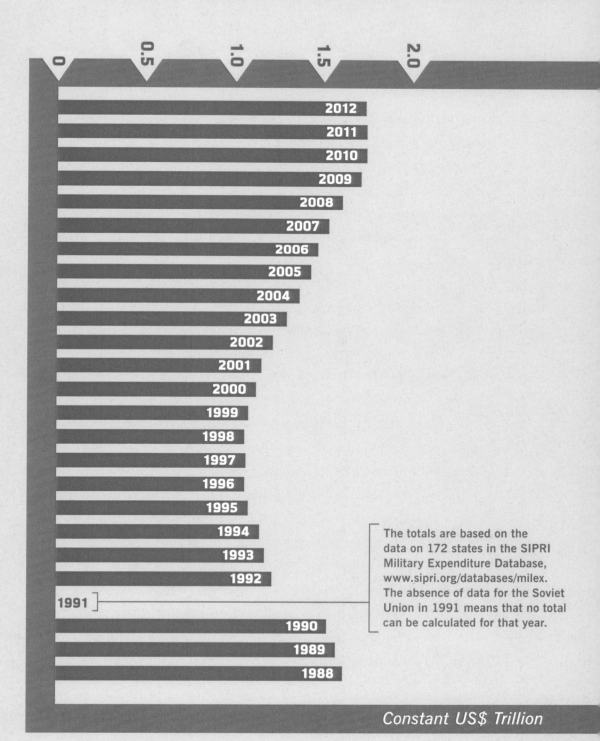

The totals are based on the data on 172 states in the SIPRI Military Expenditure Database, www.sipri.org/databases/milex. The absence of data for the Soviet Union in 1991 means that no total can be calculated for that year.

*Constant US$ Trillion*

**STAY INFORMED**

**START A CLUB**

**FACILITATE A DISCUSSION**

**EXPRESS YOURSELF**

**HOST A FILM SCREENING**

**VOICE YOUR CONCERN**

**CREATE AN EVENT**

**SIGN UP**

# 10 THINGS YOU CAN DO!

**PLAN A PRESENTATION**

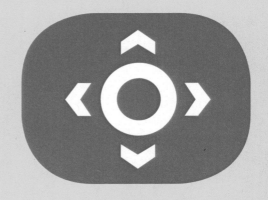

**REACH OUT**

ACTION

# ST
## INFO

# AY
## RMED

Disarmament issues provide opportunities for organizing and outreach, but as ever the first step is to become informed. Going online to find reputable sources is a good starting point. There are many useful websites where you can read the latest information on nuclear weapons, small arms and light weapons. Most of these sites have breaking news stories, regional reports, fact sheets, in-depth studies, timelines, calendars of events, and many additional links to facilitate networking and further study.

First up, to stay informed, is an exploration of the role that the United Nations plays for disarmament, followed by a select grouping of non-governmental organizations working on issues related to the arms trade and nuclear disarmament.

# DISARMAMENT AT THE UNITED NATIONS AND RELATED BODIES

The United Nations is the leading organization dealing with global non-proliferation and disarmament issues. Several UN bodies have different tasks. **The General Assembly (www.un.org/en/ga)**, where all UN Member States meet, was given the chief responsibility for considering "the general principles of cooperation in the maintenance of international peace and security, including the principles governing disarmament and the regulation of armaments".

The General Assembly has divided its work over several committees. The **First Committee (www.un.org/en/ga/first)** deals with disarmament and international security. The resolutions on disarmament that pass through this committee are taken up by the General Assembly in its plenary sessions and, once adopted, guide the agenda of the UN on specific disarmament themes.

The **UN Disarmament Commission (bit.ly/1m2ScWt)** is a more reflective body, where States discuss, not decide, on more general questions of disarmament and arms control.

The 15-member **Security Council (un.org/en/sc)**, with five permanent members, bears "the primary responsibility for the establishment and maintenance of international peace and security" in our world. The Charter also mandates the Security Council to formulate plans for the regulation of weapons and their use. The Security Council also has the power to deploy UN peacekeepers to conflict regions to prevent war and the escalation of armed violence. The Council focuses on crises, but increasingly has an eye for the root causes of conflict and war. Its resolutions are legally binding for all UN States. They can range from establishing an arms embargo on a specific country, to ensuring that terrorists do not acquire weapons of mass destruction, to setting the standards for how to tackle the small arms problem in countries coming out of conflict.

The **Conference on Disarmament (CD) (www.unog.ch/disarmament)**, based in Geneva, Switzerland, is not formally a

The "Non-Violence" (or "Knotted Gun") sculpture by Swedish artist Carl Fredrik Reuterswärd on display at the UN Visitors' Plaza in New York City.

**The Treaty on the Non-Proliferation of Nuclear Weapons (NPT) was born in 1968 out of mounting global concerns over the spread of nuclear weapons from 1945 into the mid 1960s. Under the Treaty, non-nuclear weapon States are forbidden to manufacture, possess or otherwise acquire nuclear weapons in exchange for the right to develop nuclear energy for peaceful purposes, including power generation as well as medical and industrial applications.**

**The NPT remains the only legally binding commitment to achieving a world without nuclear weapons. Every five years the Treaty is "reviewed" and progress on disarmament is assessed by States parties to the NPT. The next NPT Review Conference will provide excellent opportunities for students to get informed and get involved.**

UN body. It is the world's single multilateral forum for negotiating disarmament treaties. It was in the CD that the **Chemical Weapons Convention** and the **Comprehensive Nuclear-Test-Ban Treaty (www.ctbto.org)** were concluded. It is linked to the UN through a personal representative of the UN Secretary-General. Its meetings are also supported by the UN financially.

In New York and Geneva, the Office for Disarmament Affairs (UNODA) promotes: nuclear disarmament and non-proliferation; disarmament of other weapons of mass destruction, including chemical and biological weapons; and combatting the illicit trade in small arms and light weapons. It is responsible for implementing the decisions of the General Assembly on matters concerning disarmament. It fosters dialogue, transparency and confidence-building measures and encourages regional disarmament efforts. It also coordinates the disarmament-related work of other parts of the UN system. It supports education, research, conferences on disarmament, and engages with the public at large through publications and an interactive and informative website (**www.un.org/disarmament**).

The Vienna-based **International Atomic Energy Agency (IAEA) (www.iaea.org)** was founded in 1957 to promote the transfer of peaceful nuclear energy technology. It is a UN-related body established as an autonomous organization for safeguarding nuclear-weapon materials and the monitoring of the proliferation of nuclear technology that might be used for developing weapon systems. IAEA staff are the frontline negotiators and inspectors who oversee the development, production, stockpiling, and proliferation of nuclear-weapons-useable materials.

Also located in Vienna is the Preparatory Commission for the Comprehensive Nuclear-Test-Ban Treaty (CTBTO). While the Treaty itself has not yet entered into force, the **CTBTO** has been working to establish a global verification regime to monitor compliance with the Treaty's aims, banning nuclear explosions by everyone, everywhere: on the Earth's surface, in the atmosphere, underwater and underground. The CTBTO provides the technical support and infrastructure to ensure that a nuclear-weapon test can be detected and verified.

The Organisation for the **Prohibition of Chemical Weapons** (www.opcw.org) is the Secretariat of the **Chemical Weapons Convention (bit.ly/1eOLLy2)** that monitors compliance by States that are parties to the Convention and oversees the destruction of existing stocks of chemical weapons.

Though there is no independent international organization affiliated with the Biological Weapons Convention (BWC), the BWC bans the production, stockpiling and use of biological weapons. As a confidence-building measure, States that have signed on to the Convention exchange detailed information each year on such items as the high-risk biological research facilities that are located in their respective countries or territories.

In Geneva, the **United Nations Institute for Disarmament Research (UNIDIR) (unidir.org)** is responsible for conducting independent research on disarmament and arms control. The **Advisory Board on Disarmament Matters (bit.ly/1dJWpK7)** advises the Secretary General on matters relating to arms limitation and disarmament, and serves as the Board of Trustees of UNIDIR. It also advises on the implementation of the recommendations of the United Nations Disarmament Information Programme.

The **United Nations Mine Action Service (UNMAS) (www.mineaction.org/unmas)** of the **Department of Peacekeeping Operations (http://www.un.org/en/peacekeeping)** acts as the

 **TIP**

**A great way to keep informed of the lastest news on disarmament is to use Google Alerts (www.google.com/alerts) or Google News (news.google.com) and customize them to your interests. Google Alerts will search the web and send email updates that match your queries.**

**Most of the nuclear weapons in today's arsenal would explode with a force roughly 8 to 100 times stronger than the bombs dropped at Hiroshima and Nagasaki.**

focal point for landmine–related issues and coordinates all mine-related activities within the UN. UNMAS focuses on mine clearance, mine awareness, risk reduction education, victim assistance, advocacy, and stockpile destruction.

# NGOs AND RESEARCH ORGANIZATIONS

A non-governmental organization (NGO) is an organization independent from any government or the business sector that works at the local, national or international level to seek social change directly by funding projects or indirectly by influencing the political system. The term NGO first emerged with the founding of the United Nations and was used to distinguish national and international groups working on issues related to the UN. In terms of disarmament and non-proliferation, NGOs help influence government policy and create innovative solutions for the many problems that face us in our world. The work of NGOs often consists of: writing and research, education and outreach, media campaigns to raise awareness, and social action to create change.

Listed here is a brief annotated list of NGOs working on disarmament. Although the UN does not endorse any of these groups, their websites can be good resources where students can learn more about disarmament issues. You will no doubt realize that each website usually leads to other related projects.

# NGOs AND OTHER ORGANIZATIONS WORKING ON SMALL ARMS

**Amnesty International (www.amnesty.org):** Based in London and founded in 1961, Amnesty International is one of the most influential NGOs in the world for their campaigns on human rights. They were awarded the Nobel Peace Prize in 1977. Amnesty was a key NGO in bringing about the Arms Trade Treaty.

**ControlArms (www.controlarms.org):** ControlArms is a global civil society campaign that worked to build support for an Arms Trade Treaty. Its website is available in Arabic, English, French and Spanish.

**Human Rights Watch (www.hrw.org):** Human Rights Watch is an international NGO based in New York that works to protect human rights throughout the world.

**International Action Network on Small Arms (www.iansa.org):** IANSA brings a network of 800 grassroots organizations in 120 countries, all working to stop the proliferation of small arms and light weapons and to legislate for stricter gun control and treaties on the global arms trade.

**International Committee of the Red Cross (www.icrc.org):** The ICRC, established in 1863, works worldwide to provide humanitarian help for people affected by conflict and armed violence and to promote the laws that protect victims of war. An independent and neutral organization, the ICRC has a mandate that stems essentially from the Geneva Conventions of 1949.

**International Peace Bureau (www.ipb.org):** Founded in 1891 and based in Geneva, the International Peace Bureau has worked for a world without war through its 282 member organizations in 70 countries. In 1910 the organization received the Nobel Peace Prize. The current programme focuses on disarmament and development.

**Saferworld (www.saferworld.co.uk):** Established in 1989, working in Africa, Asia and Europe, and based in London and Nairobi, Saferworld focuses on policy research and technical support to governments and NGOs. Saferworld works to draw attention to, and to make safer, those places affected by violence and the impact of small arms and light weapons.

**Stimson (www.stimson.org):** Stimson conducts in-depth research and analysis to provide policy alternatives and to overcome obstacles to a more peaceful and secure world.

Mushroom cloud after "Fat Man" exploded over Nagasaki on 9 August 1945.

# NUCLEAR LEXICON

The Comprehensive Nuclear-Test-Ban Treaty (CTBT) bans nuclear-weapon test explosions, and all other nuclear explosions, in the air, underwater, on land, underground and in space. The CTBT was adopted in 1996 but will only enter into force when all 44 States mentioned in its Annex II have signed and ratified it. They possess either nuclear power or nuclear research reactors—8 of these States also possess nuclear weapons, and one more is believed to possess nuclear weapons. Those countries that are required and have not yet ratified the Treaty are: China, the Democratic People's Republic of Korea, Egypt, India, the Islamic Republic of Iran, Israel, Pakistan and the United States.

**The Stockholm International Peace Research Institute (www.sipri.org):** Based in Stockholm, SIPRI is an independent international institute dedicated to research about conflict, armaments, arms control and disarmament. Founded in 1966, SIPRI provides data, analysis and recommendations, based on open sources, to policymakers, researchers, media and the interested public.

**Small Arms Survey (www.smallarmssurvey.org):** Situated in Geneva, the Small Arms Survey is an independent research project that provides public information on small arms—including its authoritative yearbook—and is a highly regarded resource for governments, policymakers, researchers, and NGOs.

**Viva Rio (www.vivario.org.br):** Located in Brazil, Viva Rio works on human security and small arms disarmament throughout Latin America. It combines research with action campaigns and participatory media platforms to network and share research. Its website is in Portuguese, Spanish, French and English.

# NGOS AND RESEARCH ORGANIZATIONS WORKING ON NUCLEAR DISARMAMENT AND NON-PROLIFERATION

Painting by survivor, Kazuo Kawaguchi, of the destruction in Nagasaki, Japan, in the aftermath of the atomic bombing on 9 August 1945.

**Abolition 2000 (www.abolition2000.org):** Founded in 1995 at the Non-Proliferation Treaty Review and Extension Conference, Abolition 2000 is open to all organizations endorsing the Abolition 2000 Statement. It is a international network of over 2,000 organizations in more than 90 countries world-wide working for a global treaty to eliminate nuclear weapons. The network aims to provide groups concerned about nuclear issues with a forum for the exchange of information and the development of joint initiatives. The Abolition 2000 network meets once a year and communicates, on an ongoing basis, via a number of list serves and through conferences, teleconferencing, and periodic mailings.

**Bulletin of the Atomic Scientists (www.thebulletin.org):** In-depth information and analysis about current proliferation issues, weighing in on both nuclear weapons and nuclear energy. The journal was founded in 1945 by Albert Einstein and other prominent scientists from the atomic research and development programme called the Manhattan Project as a response to the secrecy surrounding the bomb, and the urgency for nuclear disarmament.

**Institute for Energy and Environmental Research (www.ieer. org/ensec/index.html):** IEER's Energy and Security newsletter comprises first-rate research on nuclear non-proliferation, disarmament and energy sustainability, and is available online in English, French, Spanish and Russian, with select articles in Korean, Chinese and Japanese.

**International Association of Lawyers Against Nuclear Arms (en.ialana.de):** IALANA works to prevent nuclear war and

This piece of chimney slate marks ground zero at Nagasaki. Here temperatures would have exceeded 3,000 degrees Celsius, instantly incinerating everything.

abolish nuclear weapons through implementing international law and examining nuclear policy from a legal viewpoint—with a special emphasis on the International Court of Justice decision that found nuclear weapons "generally illegal".

**International Campaign to Abolish Nuclear Weapons (www.icanw.org):** ICAN is a global grassroots campaign dedicated to engaging a new generation in nuclear disarmament. Photos, videos and teaching tools that incorporate writing, art and drama are some of the ways people are engaged to build support for a treaty banning nuclear weapons.

**International Physicians for the Prevention of Nuclear War (www.ippnw.org):** Focusing on health and medical issues, IPPNW was founded by Soviet and American doctors during the height of the Cold War. Convinced that nuclear war would be the "final epidemic", they joined together to alert the public to the dangers of nuclear weapons and radiation. In 1985, they were awarded the Nobel Peace Prize. The **Nuclear Weapons Inheritance Project (www.ippnw-students.org/NWIP/)** is IPPNW's youth project with young doctors taking action for disarmament. With a special focus on non-confrontational dialogue with nuclear decision makers, the project connects young medical professionals around the globe as they embark on their careers as healers and disarmament activists.

**Pugwash Conferences on Science and World Affairs (www.pugwash.org):** Since 1957, the Pugwash Conferences on Science and World Affairs have brought together influential policy officials, scientists and public figures to seek ways of eliminating nuclear weapons and reducing the threat of war. With its founder and then-President, the physicist Joseph Rotblat, Pugwash was jointly awarded the 1995 Nobel Peace Prize.

**Nuclear Darkness (www.nucleardarkness.org/):** A project led by Steven Starr for the Missouri Nuclear Weapons Education Fund, Nuclear Darkness is a comprehensive primer on the environmental effects of nuclear war, particularly relating to fire and climate change. Filled with a wide range of content on nuclear weapons, articles, videos and many links to other resources, this site also has a firestorm "simulator" that details what might happen in regions throughout the world if nuclear weapons were used. The website is available in English, Russian, Chinese and Hebrew.

**Nuclear Files (www.nuclearfiles.org):** The site includes an annotated history of the nuclear age reaching back to the discovery of the atom. There is also an impressive collection of archival material including photographs, video and audio recordings. An excellent resource for teachers, the Nuclear Files is a project of the Nuclear Age Peace Foundation, and is part of the National Science Digital Library.

**The Oxford Research Group (bit.ly/1doQJVs):** A United Kingdom–based think tank and dialogue centre that builds trust between policymakers, military personnel, civil society and academics, the Oxford Research Group works to address the toughest security questions using detailed research and drawing on a deep understanding of how human beings behave. Creating a sustainable security approach to counter the consequences of insecurity (such as terrorism and nuclear proliferation), the Oxford Research Group examines how current policies can better address these underlying trends rather than treat their symptoms.

**Reaching Critical Will (www.reachingcriticalwill.org):** Reaching Critical Will is the one-stop shop for basic facts on disarmament treaties, including treaty language and analysis, plus an excellent nuclear inventory tracking the countries that have nuclear power and nuclear weapon technology. Reaching Critical Will is a project of the **Women's International League for Peace and Freedom (www.wilpfinternational.org)**.

The ruins of the Urakami Cathedral. In 1945, Nagasaki was home to the largest population of Christians in all of Asia. Ninety percent of the 20,000 Catholics living in Nagasaki died from the atomic blast.

**"For decades, we believed that the terrible effects of nuclear weapons would be sufficient to prevent their use. The superpowers were likened to a pair of scorpions in a bottle, each knowing a first strike would be suicidal. Today's expanding nest of scorpions, however, means that no one is safe. The presidents of the Russian Federation and the United States—holders of the largest nuclear arsenals—recognize this. They have endorsed the goal of a world free of nuclear weapons..."**

*United Nations Secretary-General* ◀
*Ban Ki-moon, excerpt from "A five point-plan to rid the world of nuclear weapons"*

START

CL

# ÅUĐB

One way to initiate studying and discussing disarmament and non-proliferation is to start a school club, an after-school programme, or even host a youth conference. Such discussions will spark the interest of participants and encourage them to read related material to better familiarize themselves with the topics. Creating forums for discussion allows for healthy exchanges of ideas, and inspires participants to remain actively engaged. Below are some steps to help facilitate the process of starting a school club or hosting a youth conference. These steps can be useful not only for disarmament and non-proliferation but for any student club or conference about critical social and environmental issues.

**RECRUIT:** You can start a club alone, but it is better to recruit other students to help the process. Usually, a small group of students or youth leaders begins meeting informally to discuss ideas. Actively seek the support of key adults, such as a school or faculty staff member who can serve as an advisor or liaison.

**PLAN:** It is best not to rush the process of starting a youth club. In the initial stages, students should discuss and brainstorm the following:

- the purpose of the club
- possible activities
- regular meeting logistics
- outreach to other students
- short-term and long-term goals.

**CONSULT:** If possible, students should visit other school-based clubs or after-school projects to see how other groups got started, and how these established clubs are organized and run. This is a good way to see what works and what doesn't work. Usually after-school clubs need to have a description, a mission statement, or even a short constitution. Similar documents from other clubs could be very useful in understanding the form of these requirements.

**KNOW YOUR RIGHTS:** Often students have rights for holding meetings in their schools or on campus, as long as the group is student-led. You should consult with your school administration about any rules that exist for organizing clubs.

**FINANCE YOUR CLUB:** Some schools have funds set aside for student clubs and after-school activities. Check with your faculty advisor or school administrator to see what is available and what procedures must be followed to request such funds. Oftentimes, groups have to submit a proposal to receive official club status. Once achieved, clubs can use funds for meeting and promotional activities. Even a one-time youth conference

Young students in their traditional dress proudly waive their national flags during the Peace Bell ceremony of the observance of the International Day of Peace: "Peace—A Climate for Change", at UN Headquarters in New York.

 **TIP**

**Creating forums for discussion allows for healthy exchanges of ideas, and inspires participants to remain actively engaged.**

may be able to request money from a school (or a school district/department of education) for extra-curricular activities.

**PROMOTE YOUR CLUB:** Once your club or after-school programme is ready, it is time to get the word out through fliers, posters, announcements, and by word-of-mouth. Check with your school for rules (and rights) to use bulletin boards, posters, tabling in the cafeteria, announcements before classes, and handing out promotional material, etc.

**MEET:** When everything is ready, hold your first meeting and welcome everyone. Your initial meeting should be more of a social occasion where people get to know each other and to informally discuss the ideas behind the club. Don't be discouraged if your initial numbers are small or if they drop off after the first meeting. Most clubs begin small and grow. Continue to meet and promote your club and in time you'll have a "critical mass" of students.

**SPECIAL EVENTS:** As your club grows, you might begin to plan special events such as film screenings, presentations, lectures, and even a one-day or half-day youth conference. See other sections in this book on How to Host a Film Screening, How to Plan a Presentation, How to Create an Event, and How to Facilitate a Discussion.

# YOU

## CAN PARTICIPATE

in a model United Nations conference or start a club in your school. Model United Nations, also known as Model UN, is an organized simulation of the United Nations that aims to educate participants about current events, topics in international relations, diplomacy and the United Nations agenda. Many schools sponsor Model UN (MUN) as part of their extracurricular activities. If you are involved in organizing a MUN conference think about adding "disarmament" to the list of agenda items that is debated. Visit the UN4MUN website (outreach.un.org/mun) for more information about how to organize a MUN conference.

ACTION

# FACIL
# A DISCU

ITATE

SSION

Facilitating a meeting about disarmament and non-proliferation can be fun; it feels good and constructive to address challenging social issues. Once you have established your group or school club, facilitation is an important skill to acquire. From the Latin word *facilis*, which means "easy", facilitating is about helping a meeting or conversation to run smoothly. This can be accomplished, even when controversial issues are discussed, by making sure that all the participants get to contribute and be involved during the discussion. When talking about non-proliferation and disarmament issues, facilitation can help manage the discussion when there are differences of opinion and strongly held beliefs. As you think of a facilitator, think of a train conductor, with the conversation or meeting as the train. The facilitator/conductor is helping operate the train of communication and letting the passengers know what station or agenda item is coming up and if there is a delay on the line, like a difference of opinion, the conductor's job is not to comment but to guide. Here are some simple steps.

**CHOOSE A FACILITATOR:** You can do this by picking a name out of a hat or simply asking for a volunteer. Learning how to facilitate can be easy, and is an important skill in learning how to manage communication. However, if you meet regularly as a group the role of facilitator should be shared. It is far better for the process to share this role equally. The role of the facilitator is to call on people to speak and encourage involvement from the group so that everyone gets the opportunity to participate. The facilitator guides the group through the meeting from one agenda item to the next, being clear about the timetable and calling on people to speak when they wish to. The facilitator's role is not to comment on what is being said or to dominate the discussion. In fact, when someone is facilitating they forfeit their right to speak as a participant unless they call on themselves to speak outside their role. A few qualities essential to good facilitation include being

Scout leader facilitating a discussion with his troop.

- Flexible
- Non-judgmental
- Supportive
- An active listener
- A good timekeeper

**KEEP A RECORD:** If necessary, ask for a volunteer "scribe" as well. The role of the scribe or note taker is to record what takes place in the meeting, for example, action steps that need to be taken to move forward with a project and who is responsible for what.

**AGREE UPON AN AGENDA:** Ask for agenda items from the group at the beginning of your meeting. If you are meeting about a film screening you are organizing or another form of action, there are obvious items to include, such as, how is the publicity going, who is taking care of the venue selection, did the email invitation get sent, etc. If you are meeting to discuss an article you've read, the agenda items might be a list of topics to cover and people who want to comment on these. There are many ways to draw up an agenda. Just make sure that everyone gets the opportunity to be a part of the meeting, if they so choose.

# FISHBOWL PROCESS

Palestinian children discuss the importance of risk awareness in relation to unexploded ordnance.

The fishbowl process is a unique and participatory method for conducting a large group conversation that can feel like a small group. In a "fishbowl", participants practice active listening, active communication and often experience an increased understanding of a variety of viewpoints. When you are actively listening, it means you're giving full attention to whoever you are in communication with.

Likewise, active communication is a lively practice of listening and speaking in turn. The fishbowl provides a method for respectful and equal communication within a dynamic participatory experience of open discussion and dialogue.

**DIRECTIONS FOR A FISHBOWL:** Arrange the classroom seats in two concentric circles. The innermost circle is where the fish in the fishbowl get to communicate—this is where all conversation takes place. The outer circle represents the glass bowl of the fishbowl. This is where the observers sit and actively listening.

Dependent on the size of group, set up the inner circle with chairs for the participants. If there are five people as fish in the bowl, there should be seven seats. The idea is that five seats should always be occupied with two seats always empty. Once the conversation starts, anyone from the outside circle of observers can stand up and occupy one of the two empty seats inside the fish bowl. Because five seats should be occupied with two seats empty, at all times, one of the participants already in the fishbowl will have to relinquish his/her seat, and take a seat in the outside circle of observers. In this way, the conversation is shared among many different people, moving in and out of participation and observation roles.

**WRAPPING IT UP:** After the fishbowl method is used, bring all participants together, get a sense of how this communication technique worked for everyone, with a go-around.

**HERE ARE A FEW QUESTIONS THAT CAN HELP GUIDE THE DISCUSSION:**

- Was it easy to move from speaker to observer, from fish to bowl-watcher?
- Did you hear or say anything that was surprising?
- What is one thing you have learned from this experience?

**AGREE UPON A TIMETABLE FOR THE MEETING AND EACH AGENDA ITEM:** Because people have different commitments, it is important to agree upon a timetable for your meeting and assign times for each agenda item. Some of the time slots might be easy to assign, such as the introductory exercises, say for example, 10 minutes. But if the bulk of your meeting is a brainstorm or discussion then you should allocate the time accordingly. Remember that deciding on the agenda items and the timetable is a group process. This means that everyone gets to have input, if they want to.

**BEGIN WITH A CONNECTING EXERCISE:** It is always beneficial to start each meeting with some sort of connecting exercise. This might be a "go around" where each person says their name and their favorite food to eat or their favorite place to be. Simple, straightforward exercises like this can help the group settle in and feel comfortable.

**TABLING AGENDA ITEMS:** If your meeting is running late, the facilitator could ask the group for more time. If the group agrees, then the agenda can be adapted. If the group does not agree, then those agenda items that have not been covered can be "tabled" until the next meeting. Tabling agenda items means to put them on hold, and to address them at the next opportunity.

**DID YOU KNOW THAT...**

**More than 1,200 companies, in over 100 countries, are involved in some aspect of small arms production.**

**HYPES AND GRIPES: Getting to Know Your Partners.** Another great exercise is something called "Hypes and Gripes". This can also be used at the beginning of a meeting. Participants are given 1-2 minutes each, to mention something that is going well for them (a hype) and something that is not going well (a gripe). This is a wonderful way to share that remains brief but allows people to voice their concerns—and once shared, these feelings are often laid to rest. This is an especially helpful exercise for students who work together regularly. But remember, keep it brief, give yourselves a set amount of time, and stick to it.

**AGREE ON THE NEXT MEETING TIME AND CHOOSE A FACILITATOR:** It is always best to agree on the next meeting date when the group is assembled. This is much easier than trying to organize through chats in the hallway between classes, on the phone or via email. While everyone is gathered together, decide the next time and place for your meeting. It is also helpful to choose the next facilitator and that person can then be responsible for collecting agenda items and sending out a meeting reminder.

**CLOSE WITH A CONNECTING EXERCISE:** If you have time, close the meeting with a brief connecting exercise. This can work to focus the group's energy on what has been accomplished. Try a "go-around" with each person reflecting on what they've learned at the meeting.

Now that you understand the facilitation process, and have the fishbowl as an example of creative facilitation, here are a few discussion starters you might use on nuclear weapons and small arms issues. You can find more in the Overview section of the United Nations Cyberschoolbus Disarmament and Non-Proliferation education website (www.un.org/cyberschoolbus/dnp).

# NUCLEAR WEAPONS

- What is the difference between non-proliferation and total disarmament?
- Why do some Member States within the United Nations favor non-proliferation and others total disarmament?
- Why do some countries want to develop nuclear weapons?
- Which countries have nuclear weapons?
- What international treaties exist to prevent the development and use of nuclear weapons?
- Is total nuclear disarmament possible?
- Has any country ever given up its nuclear weapons?

# SMALL ARMS

- What is the difference between gun control and disarmament?
- Do only armed forces and police forces own small arms?
- Where do illegal arms come from?
- Why do people want to own guns?
- What illegal activities are often associated with the illegal small arms trade?
- Are all small arms stockpiles around the world well-guarded?
- Who are the victims of violence associated with small arms?
- What measures have been taken by the United Nations to curb small arms violence?
- What steps could the international community make to control and prevent light weapons from falling into the wrong hands?
- What is the difference between the legal and illegal trade in small arms?

## TIP

There are several options for running a discussion group. Using a fishbowl can be a great way to "facilitate" a discussion even without a facilitator.

**"What is Human Security:
Human security is far more than
the absence of violent conflict.
It encompasses human rights,
good governance and access to
economic opportunity, education
and health care. It is a concept
that comprehensively addresses
both "freedom from fear" and
"freedom from want" and is
based on a framework that
emphasizes both "protection"
and "empowerment.""**

*from United Nations Office for the
Coordination of Humanitarian Affairs
website (bit.ly/MryhW4)*  ◀

ACTION

# EXPR
# YOUR

# ESS SELF

There are numerous ways that students can express themselves and make their voices heard. You have the right to do so, especially concerning critical topics such as the proliferation of weapons and the violence associated with them. Below are some suggestions with supporting links for more information. Remember that while you will want to pick a method that best fits your personal interest and creative style you will also want to take into consideration your target audience and their needs and circumstances in order to best get your message across. There are many online guides for young people to express themselves today, for example, Adobe Youth Voices (youthvoices.adobe.com) is a comprehensive guide on how to express yourself using video, multimedia, web design, animation, and audio production.

**Here are some exciting ways of making your voice heard:**

**RADIO:** One of the most effective ways to promote your ideas about disarmament is to use local radio. There are several ways to use radio. One is to engage with local, campus radio stations—many universities and colleges broadcast from their campuses. Community radio, another excellent resource, is widespread and very popular. You can also seek out Internet-based radio stations that offer air-time for critical social issues. With any radio source, you can always reach out to existing talk shows and inquire about youth participation. There are often projects that focus on training young people to become radio correspondents. Find one near you!

Many local talk shows look for interesting subjects. You may want to invite a local producer to an event you organize in order to establish a relationship. Once a local producer becomes aware of your group, see if you can arrange an interview about your project on their radio show. Interviews can be done over the telephone but local radio shows usually invite guests into their sound studio. In addition to doing an interview yourself, you can try to arrange an interview with others in your community who have an expertise on disarmament and non-proliferation issues or someone whose life has been impacted by gun violence or nuclear issues. You may be surprised by how many people in your community have a direct link to the issues. Personal stories can make very compelling radio.

Make sure you do some research on the radio station in order to better understand its particular editorial stance. Also ask the producer how long the interview will be in order for you to prepare your notes. Make sure you have a fact sheet if necessary and resources where listeners can get more information. It's always good to practice before doing a live interview and you should keep your opening and closing remarks brief. Remember to speak clearly, slowly, and to use short sound bites to punctuate your presentation.

Many radio programmes are also live with listeners calling in, which can make for an interesting experience. Be careful not to offend any dissenting caller or to say anything you might regret in public. While speaking, try to relax, keep your cool, have a sense of humour, and do not pretend to know all the answers. Finally, remember you are representing a larger

A student with a painted face participates in a peace rally to commemorate the anniversary of the atomic bombings of the Japanese cities of Hiroshima and Nagasaki.

Some of the unexploded devices (UXL) that a United Nations Chinese battalion collected in the demining of the town of Hiniyah in Lebanon.

youth group, so stay focused on the specific disarmament issues that are being discussed.

Besides participating in a talk show format, there are also several youth media initiatives that train students to create radio stories about social issues. Radio Rookies from WNYC, a public radio station in New York, is an example of a youth radio production that can serve as a model if something like this does not already exist in your area. Through semester-long workshops, the programme trains young people to craft stories about themselves, their communities, and the larger world. Students are taught the fundamentals of radio journalism ranging from how to develop story ideas, research stories, write scripts, scout locations, record ambient sounds, conduct interviews, digitally edit their stories, and broadcast their finished pieces. You can listen to **Radio Rookies (www. wnyc.org/shows/rookies)** documentaries online.

**VIDEO:** A very effective way of promoting disarmament is through creating visual media, like making your own video. Creating a video may mean filming, editing and producing your own short film. Video files can be easily transferred from small inexpensive cameras to computers. Some of the most powerful and moving videos have been taken by amateurs who happened to be at the right place at the right time.

For more information on how to make your own video, see the video advocacy guides and resources on **Witness (www. witness.org)**, a human rights organization that specializes in video advocacy. This New York-based NGO also offers online video production training. If you want to make your own video you will need the right equipment, time and friends to help you. You can even create a video podcast or blog that you can share with people and that a wide audience can download (make sure your film is appropriate for a wide variety of audiences). Accessibility to the theme is important. As always think about the population you are trying to reach and what your message should be and the most effective way of delivering that message to your audience.

Once you've made a short film, look for places to share your work. Youtube and Vimeo offer a free means to upload videos and share with the wider global community. For juried or selected festivals, check out the Media That Matters Film Festival, an online festival for short films that highlight critical social, environmental and peace issues. There is a specific category for short films made by youth. Several of these films concern the violence associated with weapons. With no more than 12 minutes running time for each film, the pieces on Media That Matters range in style and content from animated shorts to music videos to documentaries. Now running for more than ten years, the festival attracts young independent film-makers from around the world — many are under the age of 21. The festival is guided by the principle that good, provocative films can encourage viewers to take action and become agents for social change.

**POSTERS AND BULLETIN BOARDS:** In your school there are probably numerous options for highlighting issues concerning disarmament and non-proliferation. You can design a poster, create a mural, or decorate a bulletin board. Posters can address a variety of topics associated with disarmament issues and can be bright, colorful and simple ways to get your ideas across. Posters can be made with limited resources and the materials that you need may be available right in your classroom. If you don't know where to start or you aren't sure about how to design an effective poster in order to put your message out, there are numerous Internet resources that may help to get you started. Here's a good place to begin: www.ncsu.edu/project/posters.

**T-SHIRTS:** Youth often express themselves through their clothing, buttons/badges, and especially through t-shirts. A unique design can project your message, help create group solidarity, and be an effective means of raising funds for any student organization. One-of-a-kind t-shirt designs are easy to make with online step-by-step guidelines. There are many online sites to help you create custom t-shirts. Try to find something local. You can upload your own picture or artwork or print tee shirts in your neighbourhood printmaking studio. You might consider asking other local groups where they had their t-shirts made.

 **TIP**

**Quotes from the UN Secretary-General, a disarmament expert, or a celebrity who supports this cause can add power to your message.**

**THE BIKINI BATHING SUIT:** In 1946, the French clothing designer Louis Réard, invented a two-piece bathing suit and named it after the Bikini Atoll in the South Pacific, where the United States government was conducting atmospheric nuclear-weapon tests. The famous, and at the time shocking, swimming costume was named after the results of a hydrogen bomb test, which literally split the atoll in two, inspiring Réard to invent his bathing suit, still popular today.

It is important to take into consideration that many clothes, shoes and other apparel are made in sweatshops where employment practices can be dangerous and even illegal. In some cases people are forced to work long hours in cramped environments while barely making a living wage. Furthermore, sweatshops have been known to employ children, which violates child labour laws and endangers the lives of youth. Where possible, try to source your t-shirts from ethical organizations, and you might even consider using organic cotton t-shirts, which are less harmful for the environment.

**DIGITAL STORYTELLING:** Digital Storytelling is a new term for the idea of combining pictures, personal artwork, text, or video with a sound source such as spoken word, poetry or music. You do not need to have a lot of technical computer knowledge to do this and there are numerous websites that can help you learn to create your story for people to hear and see. The Center for Digital Storytelling (**storycenter.org/stories**) has stories from students about their lives and about the issues that matter to them. You can create your own digital storytelling by using a variety of media options. Please note that if you plan to use any existing visual or written media found on the Internet, you must reference it properly or seek permission to use it. Without clear references, your expressions could be interpreted as plagiarism.

- Download **Microsoft Photo Story 3** to create slideshows using your digital photos. Add special effects, soundtracks, and your own voice narration to your photo stories (**bit.ly/1ik1iOL**).

- **Windows Movie Maker** enables you to create home movies and slide shows on your computer, complete with professional-looking titles, transitions, effects, music, and even narration (**bit.ly/1aoBIYV**).

- **iMovie for Mac** allows you to easily organize all your video clips in one place to create HD videos and trailers. To enhance your project, choose from a variety of professional templates and effects (**www.apple.com/mac/imovie**).

- **Adobe Photoshop** gives you everything you need to edit and showcase your digital images (**adobe.ly/LvnsBC**).

Over 200 kilos of unexploded ordnance (UXOs), captured from al-Shabaab militants, are destroyed outside of Mogadishu, Somalia, at a safe location.

There are many places on the Internet where images and video clips can be found and downloaded. Two good starting points are — for small arms, search the "media" archive at **IANSA (International Action Network on Small Arms — www.iansa.org)**; for nuclear issues, check out **The Bomb Project** (**bit.ly/1frlFdV**).

**BLOGGING:** Blogging has been gaining popularity over the last several years as a useful method of sharing stories and furthering knowledge both inside your immediate community and with readers all over the world. In general, blogs are concentrated on a single topic and can have either an academic or personal approach; using both can be the most compelling for the reader. Blogging can be either anonymous or attributed to yourself or your co-writers. Blogging can be posted on many websites such as facebook.com. Two of their most popular new websites for blogging are blogger.com and wordpress.com where you can pick your username, topic, and web address and then design your own site. These sites also offer a common template so you can set up your blog with little web design knowledge. Blogs on small arms and disarmament can be found at the sites listed below:

- Blog on small arms: wordpress.com/tag/small-arms

- For blogs on nuclear disarmament go to:
  bit.ly/1n8L7Eb
  disarmamentactivist.org

- On both nuclear and small arms, visit UNIDIR's blog at:
  www.disarmamentinsight.blogspot.com

**ECARDS/POSTCARDS:** You can also design innovative and creative postcards to send, using original artwork, your own photos, or search the Internet for appropriate images to use. As long as the cards are not sold commercially and used for educational purposes only, you can use online photographs. However, you must seek permission to use the images and reference accordingly.

The combination of text and images can create critical and even ironic juxtapositions. The idea here is to combine creativity and activism to call attention to the proliferation of weapons. But cards can also be an effective means of contacting public officials. Postcards can be mailed with handwritten letters to express your opinion or urge a public official to take action for disarmament. Special postcard-sized paper for ink jet printers is widely available at local office supply stores and there are many online postcard production facilities where you can upload your own picture and design. In some places, not all, these supplies are available locally. Search online for a nearby postcard production site, or partner with a local organization that can help you print your postcards.

A boy rides a bicycle past the shell of a large building, destroyed during the civil war in Angola.

ACTION

# HO
## O
### A
#### SCREEN

# ST
## FILM
### ING

Showing a film about nuclear weapons, or the proliferation and dilemmas of small arms, is a good way
to attract people to issues, spark debate, and move
people to action. A film screening can be a single
event or a series of films over a period of time. Today,
there are many traveling film festivals, as well as
festivals that are organized in school venues and
through community organizations that appeal to
youth. These festivals include feature films, documentary films, and short video essays made by
young people. Organizers can subscribe to an annual
festival, or programme their own small film series.
Two popular traveling festivals for youth that involve
issues related to human rights and social justice
include the Human Rights Watch Film Festival
(ff.hrw.org) for high schools and the Media That
Matters Film Festival (www.mediathatmattersfest.org).

Since the focus here is small arms and nuclear weapons, the list of suggested films contained in this publication is organized around these themes. To be sure, many films include or involve violence and weapons, but films where weapons are the primary subject are actually few. The list we offer is merely a short introduction to films concerning weapons. You may know of other films that focus on the proliferation of weapons that you can add to the list. Most of the films below can be easily rented or borrowed from local libraries. If this is not the case, you can always contact the filmmakers and ask them directly to loan a copy of the film or to purchase it. Organizing film festivals can be fun and engaging. Here are some steps to get you started.

**GET A TEAM TOGETHER:** Put the word out to your friends about screening a film and gather a team of interested people. Maybe you can get extra credit in a class for organizing a screening—this might be a way to get other students involved. Still, most people like to go to the movies, so getting students on-board with your idea should be easy. Make an announcement to your peers and set up a meeting time.

**FIND A VENUE:** Whether it is in your school or local theatre, the first step is to find a venue. Ask your teachers for their assistance in borrowing equipment to screen your film.

**SOLICIT LOCAL SUPPORT:** Check out your local cinema to see if there are people who would be interested in supporting your screening. You might find sympathetic adults who have access to venues and equipment outside your school and this could draw a larger, community-based audience. Use your listening and interviewing skills to help reach out to people in your community and see what happens!

**ADVERTISE YOUR SCREENING:** You can do this by putting up posters around your school, distributing flyers, sending messages to a list of email addresses you may have collected at other events you have organized, and making short announcements before your classes. Be sure to do your advertising well in advance of your screening to generate excitement and

Bullet holes mar a painting showing several adults and a child, near the Al-Basateen refugee area on the outskirts of the southern port city of Aden, Yemen.

Ammunition handed in during the 2001 voluntary buy-back campaign in Rio de Janeiro facilitated by the local NGO, Viva Rio.

interest in seeing the film! Word of mouth is often the best form of advertising.

**PRODUCE A HAND-OUT FOR YOUR SCREENING:** Students should have something to take away with them. Producing a hand-out with quotes from relevant articles, action ideas, or even something as simple as a list of websites for further information is a great take-away to keep the conversation going.

**PASS AROUND A SIGN-UP SHEET:** You should also pass around an email contact sheet for future events. This can be used for text messaging campaigns as well (see Action 10).

**FACILITATE A DISCUSSION FOLLOWING THE FILM:** Appoint a facilitator. Think of several questions that could be used as discussion starters after the screening. Where possible, invite experts or NGOs from the disarmament field or the filmmakers themselves to conduct a Q&A. Be creative. Allow time for comments from the audience.

**HERE ARE A FEW SUGGESTED FILMS:** Below are several interesting films on nuclear weapons and small arms. Given the prevalence of small arms violence in many popular films, you might want to approach these films from the perspective of three useful disarmament strategies: the desire for guns, the legal and illegal trafficking of small arms, and the situation of existing weapons in the world. These three strategies can help orient the viewers. For example, is the film more about why someone wants a gun, or is it more about the buying and selling of weapons? When screening films about nuclear weapons, be sure to review both old and new films. One useful strategy could be to ask your audience to note the change in political climate from the Cold War to the present day. You might also ask, how has the narrative about nuclear deterrence changed? Screening any of the following suggested films, both contemporary and historic, can be an exciting means of situating disarmament and non-proliferation issues in a larger teaching and learning environment. Film screenings often result in further knowledge of the subject and can generate energy for action!

# SUGGESTED FILMS ON SMALL ARMS (IN ORDER OF PRODUCTION DATE)

**AMERICAN GUN (2005).** Directed by Aric Avelino. IFC Films. This contemporary drama explores the tragedy that a gun can cause in America, even in the most affluent neighbourhoods. The intersecting story lines follow a gun shop owner, a school principal, a policeman, and the mother of a teenage killer. The outcome is a searching study on the proliferation of guns in America. For more information go to: www.americangun-movie.com

**LORD OF WAR (2005).** Directed by Andrew Niccol. Lions Gate Films. In this feature film, a Ukrainian immigrant to America makes a fortune trafficking small arms, especially Russian-made AK-47 rifles, around the world. Loosely based on real life stories of international arms dealers, the film graphically displays the effects of weapons and the global commerce of legal and illegal arms dealing. For more information go to: www.lordofwarthemovie.com

**BULLETS IN THE HOOD: A BED-STUY STORY (2004).** Directed by Terrence Fisher and Daniel Howard. Downtown Community Television (DCTV). Terrance Fisher, a teenager in the Bedford Stuyvesant section of Brooklyn witnesses a friend being shot by police. Knowing many other local teens that were also shot and killed, he decides to respond with a video camera while attending a documentary youth media course at Downtown Community Television (DCTV). Along with classmate Daniel Howard, Bullets in the Hood tells an intimate story of urban gun violence and how to process tragedy and pain in positive ways through social action and media representation. For more information go to: bit.ly/MIXOFH

**GUNS & MOTHERS (2004).** Directed by Thom Powers. Icarcus Films. Two advocacy groups, The Million Moms and the Second Amendment Sisters, are diametrically opposed on gun

A boy draws on the walls of a juvenile prison in Niger where he is being detained. The drawing depicts a man smoking a cigarette and shooting an automatic weapon.

control, but they agree on one point: mothers will and should have a voice in determining gun control policy in America. Filmed over the course of one year, starting with the Million Mom March in Washington D.C. in 2000 and the counter-rally the same day by the Second Amendment Sisters, the documentary explores the grassroots beliefs of both movements by focusing on two different women, living in two different Americas. For more information go to: **to.pbs.org/1fXLIGC**

*BOWLING FOR COLUMBINE* **(2002).** Directed by Michael Moore. MGM. Michael Moore's controversial Oscar-winning documentary about the roots of America's predilection for gun violence. Following several sensational cases, including the tragic school killings at Columbine High School, near Denver, Colorado, Moore investigates the implications for gun control. For more information go to: **www.bowlingforcolumbine.com**

*YOUNG GUNZ* **(1997).** Directed by youth participating in the Educational Video Center's filmmaking workshop. This 22-minute film focuses on New York City youth, and their powerful stories about victims of gun violence and those who admit to shooting others. For more information go to: **www.evc.org/content/young-gunz**

*LA HAINE (HATE)* **(1996).** Directed by Mathieu Kassovitz. Criterion Collection. This is a gritty, visually explosive story of what happens over the course of a single weekend when three young immigrants in the "Banlieues" outskirts of Paris find a gun. A landmark film of contemporary French cinema, *La Haine* captures the simmering social marginalization of the poorest sections of Paris, the ongoing racial tension between youth and local police, and the sudden ethical decisions one has to make when armed with a gun. For more information go to: www.criterion.com/films/216

# SUGGESTED FILMS ON NUCLEAR WEAPONS
## (IN ORDER OF PRODUCTION DATE)

*THE STRANGEST DREAM* **(2009).** Directed by Eric Bednarski. National Film Board of Canada. A moving portrait of the nuclear

physicist Joseph Rotblat, the only scientist to walk away from the Manhattan Project, the United States Government's secret wartime effort to build atomic bombs. Rotblat was awarded the 1995 Nobel Peace Prize together with the organization he created, the Pugwash Conferences on Science and World Affairs. The film also highlights current nuclear realities and the scientists and citizens who passionately work for nuclear disarmament. For more information go to:
www3.nfb.ca/webextension/strangest-dream

*WHITE LIGHT / BLACK RAIN* (2007). Directed by Steven Okazaki. HBO Films. Featuring interviews with fourteen atomic bomb survivors, many of whom had never spoken publicly before, and four Americans involved in the bombings of Hiroshima and Nagasaki in Japan, White Light/Black Rain provides a detailed exploration of the bombings and their aftermath. In a succession of riveting personal accounts, the film reveals both unimaginable suffering and extraordinary human resilience. For more information go to: bit.ly/1jbRqtA

*BLACK RAIN* (1989). Directed by Shohei Imamura. Imamura Productions. Based on the novel by Masuji Ibuse, Black Rain is a gripping movie about mankind and survival after the atomic bombing of Hiroshima in 1945. This award-winning film is an aesthetically stunning portrayal of life after the bomb and exposes how survivors struggle with radiation sickness while attempting to piece together their shattered lives. For more information go to: bit.ly/1d8hRvZ

*THREADS* (1984). Directed by Mick Jackson. BBC. This terrifying television drama is a documentary-style account of a nuclear war and its effects on the city of Sheffield in the United Kingdom. The primary plot centres on two British families as a political crisis between the USA and the USSR escalates. As the UK prepares for war, each family deal with their own personal crises. Meanwhile, a secondary plot centered upon the Chief Executive of Sheffield City Council serves to illustrate the British government's then-current continuity of government arrangements. As open warfare between the Eastern and Western military alliances erupts, the harrowing details of the characters' struggle to survive the nuclear attacks on England are rendered. The story details the fate of each family as the characters face the medical, economic, social, and

**More than 740,000 people die each year from armed violence and 490,000 of those occur outside traditional war zones.**

**OVERKILL:** Nuclear terminology describing the excessive force of a nuclear explosion. A nuclear bomb not only destroys but overkills. In other words, it carries more force than is required for total destruction. Now it is synonymous with anything thought to be excessive, as in, "that homework assignment was overkill".

environmental consequences of a nuclear war and the bleak "nuclear winter" that ensues. For more information go to: **bbc.in/1eNU5Wl**

***BAREFOOT GEN*** **(1983).** Directed by More Masaki. Madhouse Studios. This film is based on the world famous manga *Barefoot Gen* by Keiji Nakazawa, and portrays life in Hiroshima after the atomic bombing through the eyes of a child. This film encapsulates the spirit of a nation to overcome the destruction of the atomic bomb and is a testament of strength to its survivors. For more information go to: **bit.ly/1doRb5W**

***DARK CIRCLE*** **(1983).** Directed by Judy Irving, Chris Beaver and Ruth Landy. Pelican Media. Winner of the Grand Prize at the Sundance Film Festival and recipient of a national Emmy Award for Outstanding Individual Achievement in News and Documentary, *Dark Circle* follows the trail of plutonium from the Rocky Flats Nuclear Weapons facility in Colorado, to the Diablo Canyon Nuclear Power Plant in California, to Hiroshima and Nagasaki in Japan. Plutonium, the most toxic substance in the world, links these locations and the people whose lives are irrevocably changed by it. For more information go to: **bit.ly/1nOk2cO**

***ATOMIC CAFÉ*** **(1982).** Directed by Jane Loader, Kevin and Pierce Rafferty. The Archives Project. *Atomic Café* is a sometimes hilarious, sometimes sobering collection of film clips taken from American propaganda films of the 1950s. We are shown vignettes from such classic instructional films as Walt

Disney's *Duck and Cover*, wherein schoolchildren are assured that they will survive a nuclear attack simply by huddling together next to the schoolhouse wall. In another sequence, a pack of pigs are dressed in Army uniforms and left to die at "Ground Zero" during a nuclear test to see if human beings (who purportedly have the same skin consistency as pigs) could endure such an ordeal. The thrust of the production is to expose the misinformation dispensed by the government concerning the atomic bomb. For more information go to: nyti.ms/1aZleXF

**THE WAR GAME (1965).** Directed by Peter Watkins. BBC. In fifty black-and-white minutes, *The War Game* depicts the prelude to and the immediate weeks in the aftermath of a fictitious Soviet nuclear attack against Britain. The chaos of the prelude to the attack, as city residents are forcibly evacuated to the country, leads to the story's centre in Rochester, Kent, which is struck by an off-target missile aimed at RAF Manston and the Maidstone barracks. The results of that missile's explosion are the instant blinding of those who see the explosion, the resultant firestorm caused by the heat wave, and the blast front. Later, society collapses because of radiation sickness, psychological damage, and destroyed infrastructure. The British Army burns corpses, while police shoot looters during food riots. For more information go to: **pwatkins.mnsi. net/warGame.htm**

**DR. STRANGELOVE OR: HOW I LEARNED TO STOP WORRYING AND LOVE THE BOMB (1964).** Directed by Stanley Kubrick. Columbia Pictures. A dark comedy that satirizes the folly of nuclear deterrence. The story concerns an unhinged United States Air Force General who orders a first strike nuclear attack on the Soviet Union. It follows the political ramifications and back-and-forth between the President of the United States, his advisors, the Joint Chiefs of Staff, and a Royal Air Force officer as they try to recall the bombers to prevent a nuclear apocalypse. It separately follows the crew of one B-52 bomber as they try to deliver their payload. In 1989, the United States Library of Congress deemed the film "culturally significant" and selected it for preservation in the National Film Registry. For more information go to: **bit.ly/1gcj4DC**

 **TIP**

**Consider creating a social network page to continue interacting with participants after your film screening and promoting the page during your event. This can be a great way to get suggestions for future films!**

ACTION

# VOI
## YO
## CON

# CE
# UR
# CERN

Expressing your concern over the proliferation of nuclear weapons, the illicit trade in small arms and the violence associated with weapons and war is considered a basic right. The Universal Declaration of Human Rights and the UN Charter both promote freedom of expression. In a democracy, freedom of expression is crucial and elected officials are obliged to listen to their constituents. Elected officials cast votes on behalf of citizens. These votes should reflect public opinion. Hearing diverse views from citizens will help inform elected officials. Your voice is vital!

There are many ways to contact public officials. The most common way is to write a letter. Most letters are read and noted by legislators and their staff. The amount of letters received (known as a mail-count) can often influence positions. Many public officials today have personal websites and an email can also be effective means of communication especially if timing is crucial on a pending decision. An email also creates a virtual paper trail that can be useful documentation. Some politicians have their own blogs with an interactive platform for the public to respond. A phone call can also be an important means to share your concerns. Although one might not be able to speak directly to an elected official, a staff member will take the call and log the conversation. Make sure that you ask to speak with the aide who handles your issue. One can also pay officials a personal visit. Politicians may have special times set aside for scheduled lobbying appointments and even drop-in hours where anyone can visit to voice their concern.

There are several strategies for citizen advocacy clustered around a few common points. Below are five general guidelines to consider, whether it's about non-proliferation and disarmament, or any civic advocacy situation.

**BE BRIEF:** Remember to keep it short and simple. If you are writing a letter, try to keep it to one page. Address only one issue in each piece of communication. Talking points should be limited to a few essential pieces of information. Even if you make a personal visit to lobby, it is very important not to present too much information in the short time you may be given. A common outline is to clearly state the purpose of your concern, make concise key points, present any supporting documentation, and if your communication pertains to a specific piece of legislation, identify it, and stress how the legislation will personally impact you, or your community.

**BE ACCURATE:** Legislators have many things they are concerned with at any given time. So make certain that you are relaying concise and accurate information. The purpose for writing or communicating should be stated up front. Know the issue. If there's a specific piece of legislation, make sure you correctly identify it and state clearly the action you are

Scores of civilians, including children, have lost their limbs to landmines around the world.

advocating for. If you have any direct experience associated with the legislation, this can add credibility to your position.

**BE COURTEOUS:** Whether you agree or disagree with your legislator, you should always be courteous. Your goal as an advocate is to create a space where your legislator can consider different opinions. If you visit in person, never raise your voice and always remain patient. Do not hesitate to ask a specific question, even about your legislator's feelings towards a particular issue. Be prepared to answer questions about your own position. It is also very important to listen to your legislators and to try to understand their positions. Finally, thank your legislator for taking the time to consider your opinion.

**FOLLOW-UP:** Be sure to leave your personal contact information with your legislator or their staff. This is especially important if you are one of their constituents. Leaving your contact information allows your legislators to follow-up with you personally, but following-up is also your responsibility. Send a thank-you letter that outlines the different points covered during the meeting, reiterating any commitments he or she has made and enclose additional information that might strengthen your advocacy.

**DEVELOP A RELATIONSHIP:** Whether your legislators support your position or not, it is extremely helpful to contact them on a regular basis. Building relationships with public officials is crucial if you want to influence change. Public advocacy is a process, an ongoing conversation that involves the development and the maintenance of positions. An advocate's job is to develop a working relationship with elected officials and their staff who are assigned to work on particular issues. When it comes time for action, relationships can help influence decisions. The key is to develop a network that can make your position heard, and always maintain a respectful disposition.

**SAMPLE LETTERS:** Following the above guidelines, compose a short and courteous letter. Begin with the aim clearly stated in the opening paragraph, then include a few reasons why you are advocating your position, at least one source backing up your argument, and a call for action. Be sure to include your contact information. What follows are a few sample letters regarding the proliferation of small arms and nuclear disarmament.

# THIS IS A BRIEF SUMMARY OF THE STEPS INVOLVED IN BRINGING THE UNITED NATIONS ARMS TRADE TREATY (ATT) INTO FORCE:

**STEP 1:** The terms of the ATT were adopted by the UN General Assembly in April 2013. It is important to remember that a treaty does not enter in force when it is adopted. It must be ratified by countries through their internal legislative processes in order to become legally binding.

**STEP 2:** Once a treaty has been adopted, it is "open for signature" for a limited period of time. The ATT is open for signature for all States, until it enters into force. Thereafter, a State can still join the treaty by informing the UN of its intention to be bound by it. A treaty can be signed by a Head of State or Minister of Foreign Affairs, or other individuals, like ambassadors, who have been authorized to sign. The signing of a treaty is often accompanied by a big ceremony in order to build momentum and worldwide interest. When a country signs a treaty, it is indicating its willingness to be bound by the terms of that treaty.

**STEP 3:** A country is not legally bound by the treaty until it ratifies it. In order to ratify a treaty a country must determine if the terms of the treaty are in conflict with its existing laws or not. When a treaty conflicts with national law, then the country has to modify its laws to remove the conflict. Needless to say, this can take a while. That is why there are rarely time limits set on the ratification process.

**STEP 4:** Once the treaty has been ratified by the government, it must deposit what is called an Instrument of Ratification. In the case of the ATT these instruments are deposited with the UN Secretary-General.

**STEP 5:** Each treaty states how many countries must deposit an instrument of ratification or accession in order for the treaty to enter in force. According to the ATT, a minimum of 50 countries must ratify it in order for it to enter into force.

## TIP

**Before contacting public officials, identify your strongest argument and use it to drive your overall message forward.**

# LETTER #1: ARMS TRADE TREATY

**This letter is structured around the idea that any given country has or has not signed the Arms Trade Treaty. Check to see if your country has signed and ratified the ATT at www.un.org/ disarmament/ATT.**

Dear Representative [Name]:

We are a group of students [name school and location] studying the arms trade around the world.

▶ **OPTION A:** *For a student from a country that has not signed the ATT.*

We are surprised that our government has not signed the Arms Trade Treaty. The unregulated arms trade between countries leads to so many problems. Weapons easily fuel conflict, they are tools for human rights abuses, they hinder delivering food to the poor, they threaten those who help refugees, they terrorize children and civilians. This must be stopped, and you can make a difference. We urge you to sign the Arms Trade Treaty, which will bring responsibility to the global arms trade.

▶ **OPTION B:** *For a student from a country that has signed the ATT.*

As a signatory of the ATT, we urge you to encourage other Member States to follow your good example. The Arms Trade Treaty will bring responsibility to the global arms trade, and will save lives of people everywhere in the world.

▶ *The following can be included in either version of the letter.*

One of the things we have learned is that many weapons start out legal and are sold from one country to another, but they end up being sold again to arms traffickers who illegally ship the guns into conflict situations. Small arms that are illicitly sold can also fall into the hands of criminals. Several studies have shown that excessive amounts of weapons can increase lethal violence and remain a serious problem for years to come.

The amount of deaths associated with in particular small arms and light weapons is a global tragedy, so we decided to do something about it. We have started a letter-writing campaign to call attention to the irresponsible arms trade and to ask legislators to support the Arms Trade Treaty. We would like to know if you will support our campaign and let other officials know what is going on, so they can take action and help to prevent armed violence.

If you have any questions, you can call us [number], or you can write to us [address]. We are not going to give up on this! We want to live in a safer world. Thank you.

Concerned high school student,
[Name]

# LETTER #2: NUCLEAR WEAPONS

This letter focuses on the Treaty on the Non-proliferation of Nuclear Weapons (NPT). There are two versions, one for students living in countries that possess nuclear weapons and another for those living in countries that do not possess nuclear weapons. The NPT is the only legally binding, global agreement, with the goals of nuclear non-proliferation and nuclear disarmament. There are three big countries that stand outside the NPT: India, Israel and Pakistan. The Democratic People's Republic of Korea announced its withdrawal from the Treaty in 2003 and its legal status in the Treaty remains uncertain. If you live in a country that is not a member of the NPT, the sample letter below can be adapted and sent to an appropriate government official.

Dear Representative [Name]:

We are a group of students [name school and location] studying the Treaty on the Non-proliferation of Nuclear Weapons (NPT) and are wondering what progress is being made on implementing Article 6 of the NPT, which states that:

"Each of the Parties to the Treaty undertakes to pursue negotiations in good faith on effective measures relating to cessation of the nuclear arms race at an early date and to nuclear disarmament, and on a treaty on general and complete disarmament under strict and effective international control."

▶ **OPTION A:** *For a student from a country with nuclear weapons.*

What exactly is our country doing to work towards the abolition of its nuclear arsenal?

▶ **OPTION B:** *For a student from a country without nuclear weapons.*

What exactly is our country doing to demand that countries with nuclear weapons eliminate their nuclear arsenals?

▶ *The following can be included in either version of the letter.*

We believe that the world would be a much safer place without nuclear weapons. According to a statement by the Secretary-General of the United Nations, nuclear weapons, coupled with global climate change, represents the greatest threat known to humanity. Secretary-General Ban Ki-moon has suggested a five-point plan to implement nuclear disarmament, and one of his points is for countries with nuclear weapons to abide by their Article 6 obligations.

We understand that the road to the total elimination of nuclear weapons may be long and may be difficult, but we expect immediate steps to be taken towards this goal. We have started a study group at our school to call attention to the dangers of nuclear proliferation. We hope to discuss your response to our letter at an upcoming meeting.

If you have any questions, you can call us [number], or you can write to us [address]. The fate of our world rests upon those in power to push for nuclear disarmament and make it a reality within our lifetime.

Concerned high school student,
[Name]

ACTION

CRE
AN

# ATE
# EVENT

Activism for disarmament is often strengthened by public events. A well-timed event can disseminate information for awareness, crystalize different but related issues, mobilize people into social movements, raise money for projects, create new networks of interested groups, make visible the critical issues, promote upcoming events, as well as educate and train people to become agents for social change.

Below are several different kinds of events that are common activities in education circles. A well-planned event includes an overall strategy with various components, such as objectives, larger goals, intended audiences, messages, resources, challenges, tactics, and evaluation.

**TABLING:** One way to attract attention to non-proliferation and disarmament is to set up a table in a public space and simply talk to people and disseminate relevant information. This activity is commonly referred to as tabling. A cafeteria during lunchtime or a common hallway inside a school is always a great space for tabling. Make sure permission for setting up your table is approved by school authorities. Sidewalks can also be effective locations. Again make sure you obtain permission, in advance, to set up your table in a particular location whenever it is required. It is important to identify public venues where, at certain times of day, there is a lot of foot traffic past your table. Tables should be well marked with a banner or large lettering on poster board to communicate the topic of your display or any messaging you have created. This is especially important if your table is competing with others in the same space.

Tables should be staffed with students or advocates who have knowledge of the issues. We advise studying the various issues related to disarmament and non-proliferation because sharing information, answering questions, dialoguing over the issues, debating various points of view, and educating others are all key activities at the table. It is also important to have materials or something that students or the general public can take away.

"Take-aways" can include leaflets, fact sheets, flyers, postcards, and one-page descriptions of disarmament issues, important facts and actions you would like others to take. A successful table can lead to other events. A calendar of upcoming activities or key dates for disarmament activism should be included as well as a contact sheet in order to send out additional information or keep people informed about future events.

**TEACH-IN:** School-based events are often organized around teach-ins. These events are usually planned in advance and everyone knows the time and place. Teach-ins often involve faculty or invited speakers to make a presentation or show a video or short film about disarmament issues to spark a discussion. Other ways to structure teach-ins are to have a panel discussion, a debate, or a workshop with the intention of educating your fellow students. Students may also decide to speak. Look at *Action 9: Plan a Presentation!* for more details.

The "Art for Peace" contest is sponsored by the United Nations Office for Disarmament Affairs and the Harmony for Peace Foundation. Children were encouraged to create an original artwork using their imagination to show a world free of nuclear weapons, without bombs, wars and fear. This artwork is from 12-year-old Yin Ling of Malaysia (unartforpeace.org).

**DEMONSTRATION/RALLY:** A public demonstration or a rally is a public gathering of people to demonstrate or display a shared message in support of disarmament strategies. Demonstrations are sometimes spontaneous gatherings, but a rally is usually planned. Although demonstrations, and especially rallies, are held by people physically in a public space, demonstrations can also occur online in a virtual public space.

Activists use peaceful, non-violent demonstrations and rallies to announce their commitment to a cause, to raise awareness, to support a larger social movement, to protest perceived injustice, to make their voices heard, and to make a public call for change. Non-violent and non-destructive acts of protest are ultimately the most persuasive. Methods of protest in demonstrations and rallies include public assemblies, announcements, keynote speeches, protest songs, handing out petitions, displaying activist art, and making a concerted call for change. The messages in a demonstration can be directed towards the greater public, the media, political leaders, or people most affected by the issue.

**VIGIL:** A vigil is usually a quiet night-time event. Traditionally, vigils were meant for spiritual devotion and observance. Today, vigils are organized to offer support, show political solidarity, mourn a tragic event, and display remembrance. Vigils often involve the lighting of candles to symbolically call attention to an event or a larger issue. Many disarmament events are held as vigils to remember the victims of armed violence and war. These events can be timed to correspond with certain symbolic dates, such as, the UN International Day of Peace observed every year on September 21 or annual vigils held on August 6 and 9 to remember the atomic bombings of Hiroshima and Nagasaki.

**MARCH/PROCESSION:** A march or a procession in relation to activism simply signifies people walking in the same orderly direction for a reason. Political marches have a long and varied history such as the famous marches during the Civil Rights Movement led by Dr. Martin Luther King, Jr. in the United States or the non-violent marches led by Mahatma Gandhi in India. Activists have traditionally marched to call attention to the need for nuclear disarmament, the prevention of gun violence, and the commemoration of tragic events that have become social landmarks.

Processions can be quite impressive with marchers carrying signs and banners. People often play music and sing as they walk. Sometimes protesters carry personal items such as family photos of those who have died in war or violent conflict, and people sometimes dress in symbolic ways to project a message. A formal procession can be a powerful means to spread a message across a larger landscape. People often join processions en route. This can be an effective means of recruiting new advocates for disarmament campaigns. Although marches sometimes move through hostile territory or areas rife with potential conflict, demonstrations that are non-violent are always most effective.

**CONCERT/PERFORMANCE:** Another good way to bring attention to disarmament and non-proliferation is to hold a concert, a poetry/spoken word reading, theatre or dance performance. The combination of activism and the arts has been around for a long time and is often used to garner media attention and is another means of creating a concerned community.

In Rio de Janeiro, Brazil, there is a series of monthly concerts called Urban Connections where the best hip hop groups in the city come together in a different favela community each month to perform a free concert and talk directly to the audience about non-violence, peace, and small arms disarmament in their community. Any group of young people can organize an arts event as a benefit for a cause or as a means of addressing an audience on key disarmament issues.

Street theatre is another example of performance that is effective in bringing disarmament issues to a wide audience. As indicated in the name, street theatre is a performance form that takes place in public spaces, often outdoors and usually free. Theatrical pieces can be performed in city parks, on street corners, in school parking lots or anywhere that traffic is not obstructed and permission can be granted. Sometimes street theatre can be incorporated into planned demonstrations, block parties or festivals. To organize your production get a group together and brainstorm ideas about what you want to convey. Write a script and make sure you keep the logistics simple, such as costumes and props, because your back stage and center stage is the street.

In Toronto, Canada, the Children's Peace Theatre integrates peacemaking with theatre practices to help young people to

*continued from opposite page*

**breakdancing, beat box and rap. This resolution of conflict became a revolution in culture. Although hip hop and its music would later be associated with the gang violence it once sought to quell, music and dance were successfully used to bring people and communities together.**

# NUCLEAR LEXICON

**CRITICAL MASS:** the smallest amount of fissile material needed for a sustained nuclear chain reaction. This phrase is also used today to refer to the minimum amount (of something) required to start or maintain a venture.

engage their creativity and compassion to evolve conflict into resolution. Using theatre can engage a wide audience and, as an education tool for disarmament, both the performers and the audience get to learn and grow.

**ATHLETIC EVENT:** Organizing an athletic event can be an empowering way to raise awareness of the proliferation of weapons. An event can be a road race for runners, a summer midnight basketball league, a beach volleyball tournament, a football (soccer) match, or any other sporting event where non-proliferation and disarmament issues are made manifest. In London there is a project called Fight for Peace where young men and women participate in a boxing academy and simultaneously study human rights. In Eastern Europe, the Peace Race is a bicycle tournament that started in 1948 to bridge warring countries in the aftermath of World War II. The event is still annually staged and is an effective means of creating transnational dialogue, a purpose it served especially well during the Cold War. Athletic events have the potential to generate media and community attention. They also send an uplifting message that people can care about disarmament initiatives while doing something healthy in the spirit of solidarity.

**HOLD A SCHOOL CEREMONY:** The United Nations' Cyberschoolbus (www.un.org/cyberschoolbus/dnp) has developed a series of lessons and workshops for disarmament and non-proliferation education. A class that uses the curriculum can hold a special ceremony to recognize their efforts. New knowledge can be displayed on school bulletin boards. Other classes can be invited to the final presentations. If research projects have been conducted, these can be presented to the wider student body and faculty in a school-wide assembly. Spreading the new learning around to the entire school can also allow for questions to emerge from other classmates. In short, participating students can share their findings, their ideas for social change, and recruit new students to become activists for disarmament.

**PLAN AN INTERNET EVENT:** Using the Internet to advertise and even to host an event is a growing trend in communication and in outreach. You can create an event on various social networking sites, blogs and twitter accounts. This gives people the opportunity to join your cause and spread information on small arms and nuclear disarmament worldwide. One of the advantages to creating a group or event on one of these sites is the huge number of people you have the potential to reach. People may find your group or cause by accident or you may gain membership through directed searches of the website. Either way you have the potential to reach a global online audience and make new friends from many different countries that are interested and active in the same issues that matter to you. See Action 10 for more information on starting a virtual campaign.

**START A DISARMAMENT CAMPAIGN:** The creation of a well-planned disarmament campaign is usually the work of NGOs partnering with public officials, disarmament experts and concerned members of civil society. However, young people have started disarmament campaigns themselves. In 1997, university students in Sao Paulo, Brazil, created a successful volunteer hand-over campaign for weapons known as Sou da Paz (www.soudapaz.org). In three months, they collected 3,500 small arms working with local NGOs. We advise studying the history of disarmament campaigns. You can read about many small arms campaigns at the International Action Network on Small Arms (www.iansa.org) and nuclear disarmament campaigns at the International Campaign to Abolish Nuclear Weapons (www.icanw.org). Check these and other sites for materials you might be able to use in your own campaigns.

 **TIP**

To ensure that your event will go smoothly, gather some of your friends to help with the planning process and delegate specific roles and responsibilities so that everybody can contribute! Don't forget to collect email addresses from people attending your events so that you can send them information about future activities that might be of interest.

ACTION

# SIGN

# UP

▲

Social movements are most successful when engaging in appropriate modes of action. Action can be defined by taking the knowledge you have about nuclear weapons, small arms and light weapons and using this knowledge to advocate for change. One important way to take action is to join others so that a larger collective voice can speak together. People can mobilize with others physically in demonstrations, rallies, marches, and teach-ins. But people can also mobilize virtually by signing petitions.

A petition is a list of names and addresses of people who are demanding action on a particular issue. By seeing a long list of names of those who agree on an issue, elected officials and legislators should be moved to act on behalf of the public. In fact, some countries will only act on a particular law when a formal petition exists. For example, in 1982 at the 2nd Special Session on Disarmament, 29 million signatures were collected by civil society in support of nuclear disarmament and delivered to the United Nations. In 2003, Brazilian civil society gathered over a million signatures on a petition that led to stronger gun control laws.

Signing petitions is relatively simple but you need to fully comprehend what you are signing. Most petitions have leading paragraphs explaining the nature of the advocacy campaign. Read the petition yourself and if you do not understand it, do not sign it. Also if you are indifferent to a particular issue, refrain from signing until you have more information. But if you do understand the petition, then you can decide if you want to sign on.

If you agree on a petition's stance, sign your name where indicated. Most petitions provide space for you to print your name and your full mailing address. This is important if your petition is linked to an act of legislation because public officials can gauge how their constituents feel on a particular issue based on their geographic location.

The Million Faces and the I Love Campaign are two interesting examples of successful petitions, one on small arms and one on nuclear disarmament.

**THE MILLION FACES PETITION:** In 2003, Amnesty International, International Action Network on Small Arms (IANSA) and Oxfam International came together to create a global campaign called ControlArms. The campaign was launched in 50 different countries and received significant media attention. A goal of ControlArms was to build support among countries for an Arms Trade Treaty. The campaign encouraged governments to develop, strengthen, and enforce national and regional arms controls measures and agreements. It also worked to build partnerships between civil society groups and governments to reduce the demand and availability of small arms.

United Nations sponsored disarmament advocacy in Juba, South Sudan.

**TIP**

If you are
looking to
reach the
most people
possible, try
starting your
petition online.
Change.org is
an example of
a free online
service that
allows you to
post petitions.

The ControlArms (www.controlarms.org) website lists upcoming events, breaking news, fact sheets, media essays, studies and reports, and many related links. One of the main components of their public advocacy campaign was the Million Faces Petition which used photo portraits instead of signatures. The goal of this campaign, which was achieved, was to collect one million images of individuals around the world who support the ControlArms campaign. While it is no longer active, it was a creative way of engaging people in an issue and provides a good model for future campaigns. Check their site for information about current campaigns.

**The 'I Love' Campaign:** On a local and much smaller level, there is a group of high school students from Nagasaki, Japan, who work to collect signatures in support of nuclear disarmament. Every year representatives from this group travel to the Conference on Disarmament at the United Nations in Geneva and present their signatures to the Ambassadors at the conference.

The signature campaign originated in Nagasaki over ten years ago, but in the last five years they have started to do something they call the I Love Campaign. They have created a postcard, which has the letter "I" next to a big red heart that means "love", and next to this is a blank space. Instead of signing a petition against nuclear weapons, they have created this simple format for people to identify what they love.

The process of connecting people to places and things that they love can be an inspiration to continue to work for nuclear disarmament. Instead of signing against nuclear weapons, the students ask people to sign for something or someone in the world that they love. For the Nagasaki High School students signature campaign, it is not about what people fear but what people love that motivates change. What do you love?

Child soldiers have been extensively used in civil wars in Africa.

ACTION

# PL

# PRESEN

# AN
## A
## TATION

The United Nations Office for Disarmament Affairs website (www.un.org/disarmament) has thousands of documents about disarmament and non-proliferation that can be used as resources to help you plan your presentation. Have a look where you can find speeches by UN officials. Use the speeches as a starting point to decide what is most important to you. Speeches are interesting documents because they are often dynamic and written with the bias of spoken delivery.

Writing and making presentations can be a lot of fun and can help you learn more about a subject and share your insights with an audience. Here are a few tips on how to write a speech and how to deliver a presentation.

**CHOOSE A TOPIC/RESEARCH YOUR CHOICE:** The most important part of planning a presentation is to find something you believe in and feel passionate about. It is also important to know the latest news or any recent reports on your topic. The more you educate yourself, the more prepared you will be to make a presentation. For example, the issue of small arms is a large subject and you might look at the **International Action Network for Small Arms (www.iansa.org)** web portal to choose any of their key issues as a topic to focus on. You can also choose a geographic area within the IANSA site to make a presentation on regional issues. The more focused you are on a specific topic, the stronger your presentation will be. So the first step is to choose a subject and study it. Go to *Action 1: Stay Informed* for a list of disarmament and non-proliferation resources you can consult.

**DEVELOP A PRESENTATION PLAN:** Once you've chosen a subject, and researched your presentation as much as you can, it is best to develop a plan for your presentation. Good presentations make a few strong points to support an argument. When you search for a topic, be sure it is something you can "break down" into manageable portions. It is important to be both substantive and succinct. In other words, a good presentation has some depth to support the major points. However, try not to repeat yourself and don't try to cover too much.

As you research your specific points, remember that not everything on the Internet is trustworthy or even factual. In doing your research, it is important to look at your sources and follow the links to the original document. Think of yourself as an investigator, snooping out the appropriate people and organizations with reputable information. And why not try your school or local library? You can also conduct a survey or interview people about your topic. For example, you might ask people their opinion about nuclear disarmament, using quotes from their responses to illustrate your presentation. You might

A member of a performing troupe holds a poster showing different signs that warn of the presence of landmines, at Boeng Prolith Primary School, Cambodia.

▲

# NUCLEAR LEXICON

**FIRESTORM:** Light, heat, blast and radiation are some of the primary effects of a nuclear explosion. The immense light and thermal heat (comparable to the interior of the sun) that result from a nuclear explosion initiate phenomena called firestorms. Firestorms deplete oxygen from the environment and create hurricane-like winds, which attract debris and feed the storm itself, causing super-infernos. The word is now used to describe any controversy, as in, "there's a firestorm brewing in the city's threat to raise bus and subway fares".

even find a person who is an expert in the field. An interview with him or her can further enhance your research.

When writing up your presentation, it can be helpful to find the words of others to underline your points. In the speech by peace activist and Nobel Laureate Jane Addams, she said, "Action indeed is the sole medium of expression for ethics." Quotes from inspiring people, from the present or long ago, can help validate the points you are making.

As soon as you have enough material for a presentation, you can organize it around several key areas. First, you might give a brief introduction about your topic and explain why you are personally interested in this subject. Some presenters like to pose an overarching question or problem statement that your research will respond to. Perhaps you can add a brief section about why this particular issue needs to be talked about and studied. If there's any existing literature in your chosen field, you might mention it or reference it as you move into your key points. Present your points with research or quotes to substantiate your opinion. Remember to summarize your points and offer a short conclusion.

**PRACTICE YOUR PRESENTATION:** Write up your speech and practice reading it over and over. Ask your friends to listen to you and make eye contact with them as you read. Familiarize yourself with the points you make and the progression of your arguments. Listen for the natural rhythm of your voice and notice what points you make with the inflection of your voice and body language. Some people like to read their speech in front of a mirror. But no matter how you prepare, the more familiar you are with your text, the easier it will be to deliver it. Another key aspect of practicing is timing your presentation to see how long it takes you to do it. If, for example, you are given 15 minutes, you need to practice your presentation to make sure it stays within the time allotted. If your talk is too long, then you have to adjust and make it shorter.

**SUMMARIZE YOUR PRESENTATION:** Once you have written your talk, and have practiced it to the point where you are quite familiar with the issues and your arguments, you might want to summarize your sections and key talking points onto index cards to help guide your presentation. Some people feel more comfortable reading their paper, but it is often more effective to speak as if your presentation were extemporaneous.

Extemporaneous speaking means to speak informally, to ad-lib from your own experience and to be comfortable in your speaking manner. Write down your outline and key phrases from your written speech. Most people need to look at their index cards to make sure they are staying on point and their presentation is covering all the issues. But no matter how much you need to look at your notes, try to deliver your speech in a way that you do not appear to be reading entirely from your text. Index cards with an outline of your talk can help you deliver your message in a relaxed and natural manner.

**DELIVER YOUR PRESENTATION:** Arrive early so you have time to greet your audience as they arrive. Isn't it a positive feeling to be greeted when you first arrive somewhere? A simple hello can be a very connecting activity. Greetings can help make people feel comfortable, especially if they are coming to a new place for the first time. And it is "contagious" too. Once you start saying hello, then other people join in and soon you've got a full room that is buzzing with community. A relaxed audience is often a more receptive audience.

 **TIP**

**Some speakers find it useful to write down key words and phrases on note cards and use them as reminders to help guide their presentation.**

**START WITH GRATITUDE:** One of the first things you want to do is say a word of thanks. So you might thank your school or faculty if they helped to provide the space, or friends and teachers who helped you to write or practice your speech, or experts you may have interviewed through your research. There is always someone who has helped and for that it is wonderful to say thank you.

**CONNECT WITH YOUR LISTENERS:** Some people might think that if you are giving a speech in front of a big audience, or even a medium-sized audience, group interaction should not be encouraged. Even if you are speaking to 500 people (or more!), you can always introduce interaction and it works to engage your audience right from the start. For example, if you are talking about small arms, at the appropriate place in your speech, ask your audience to turn to their neighbour and share, for two minutes each, what they know about the violence associated with the proliferation of small arms and light weapons. Have they seen a gun? Do they know anyone who has been a victim of gun violence? How does gun violence make them feel? Be sure to keep an eye on the clock and tell your audience when each person's time is up. There are many ways to engage your audience. Group interaction can be very positive. Just make sure you reign in the energy and bring everyone back together to continue listening to your prepared remarks.

**ENJOY YOUR PRESENTATION:** People are affected when presenters are passionate about their topic. Make eye contact with your audience. Don't forget to breathe. Smile. Check your notes to make sure your presentation is moving along and you are not forgetting anything. Near the end, try to conclude your talk with a few summarizing points. Don't forget to thank the organizers and your audience, once again. If possible, it is always wise to leave time for questions and comments.

A woman walks past a sign prohibiting weapons as she enters the grounds of a regional hospital during the civil conflict in Côte d'Ivoire.

ACTION

REA

O

# 10

Many young people today are becoming politically active over the Internet and with new media technologies. These technologies can be a very effective tool for widespread communication about disarmament issues. Youth activists are using email, online petitions, blogs, Facebook, Twitter, instant messaging, and social networking sites to raise awareness and take action. Below are some suggestions on new media activism.

**PLAN AN INTERNET EVENT OR CAMPAIGN:** Using the Internet to advertise and even to host an event is a growing trend in communication and in outreach. You can create an event on popular social networking sites like Facebook and have people join your cause, or spread information on small arms and nuclear disarmament worldwide on other social networking sites like Weibo (popular with Chinese-speaking users) and Orkut (popular in Brazil and India).

Google has also created some useful tools for you to use. Once you set up a Google+ account, you can create an event on Google+ and invite others to join your event or use Google+ Hangouts to hold virtual meetings and share documents with others that are working on the same campaign. It is a useful way to stay connected. You can visit the UN Google+ account at: **bit.ly/1jbSvS3**.

One of the advantages to creating a group or event on one of these sites is the huge number of people you have the potential to reach. People may find your group or cause by accident or you may gain membership through directed searches of the website. Either way you will be able to reach a global online audience and make new friends from many different countries who are interested and active in the same issues that matter to you.

Before you get started, look at other successful campaigns on social networking sites. Here are some tips to consider:

Secretary-General Ban Ki-moon (seated) sends a Twitter message at an event in Mexico City to promote "WMD–We Must Disarm", a 100-day multiplatform campaign leading up to the International Day of Peace on 21 September 2009.

1. Write a welcome message that clearly tells those who are interested in joining your cause what you expect them to do.

2. Describe the goals and objectives clearly and succinctly.

3. Design or use a powerful image that captures what your campaign is about.

4. Post videos, digital stories (*see Action 4: Express Yourself*), or interviews you have done.

5. Encourage members to contribute content. Campaign topics and key messages can be spread through the use of hashtags (#) among Twitter and Instagram users to make the messages searchable.

6. Set goals that require the assistance of those who have joined your campaign. For example, try and recruit a specific number of members by a certain date.

7. Keep updating the content on your cause page. Many event sites allow you to insert "countdowns" towards the date and time of your event. Facebook, for instance, has a live animated countdown you can share with others.

8. Invite all your friends to join and ask them to spread the word about your event to their list of friends.

9. Find other campaigns that have similar objectives to yours and write to the creator or administrator to ask them for support.

**EMAIL:** Students who do not yet have personal email accounts can use free email services like Gmail provided by Google (mail.google.com), which is the most widely used web-based email provider. Once a Gmail account is set up, you gain access to other Google applications, such as Google Drive to create documents, presentations and spreadsheets, and Google Fusion to visualize data. Google account users also have the option of connecting their Google accounts to other social media platforms such as YouTube. Information on how to sign up is easily accessible on the web and services are available in many different languages.

Another email service for you to consider is **BluMail (bluworld.org)**—a global email, education, networking, jobs, entrepreneurship and activism portal for millions who are coming online in developing countries. BluMail offers educational content focused on conflict resolution, early childhood education, entrepreneurship, the environment, healthy lifestyles, human rights, religious understanding, women's empowerment, world knowledge and youth leadership.

**TEXT MESSAGING CAMPAIGNS:** Mobile phones are increasingly being used to launch text messaging campaigns. Text messaging campaigns are good tools for distributing information quickly, gathering information and collecting virtual signatures for a petition.

There are a few ways to use mobile phones in text messaging campaigns that do not require a big budget. One simple way is to set up a text blasting/bulk messaging system that allows you to send a single message to a group of people. For example, you can send a text message alert about an educational event on smalls arms and nuclear disarmament you are organizing to all of the phone numbers in your contacts list.

It is important for you to think about how you would create and maintain your list of phone numbers. In many places it is illegal to send unsolicited text messages. This means you will need to get permission to send messages to those you want to include in your list and have a way for them to opt out of getting messages at some later point if they so choose. Recruit people for your mobile list at events you organize. It is often the best way to sign people up.

There are other interesting ways people are using mobile phones as an important element in their campaigns. Try using the keywords such as "mobile phones + social change", "mobile phone activism", or "SMS mobile phone campaign". See what you find and think about how it can be applied to raising awareness about the arms trade and nuclear disarmament.

**INSTANT MESSAGING (IM):** Staying in touch with people who share similar interests is often done via instant messaging. This is a service that allows you to communicate over the Internet with text or voice. Many IM programmes are available for free and can be easily downloaded over the Internet.

With millions of smartphone users around the world, the great majority use their phones for messaging as well. Mobile applications allow users to connect with each other via text messaging, voice and video calling as well.

Trends for mobile applications shift quickly, so it is important to stay informed of what is the best platform to use to reach your target audience when you are ready to launch your campaign. Don't forget to check what popular messaging applications are used in other countries/regions around the world. Find someone to translate your campaign's message into other languages so that you can post messages on these applications and increase your reach around the world.

**TWITTER:** Twitter was initially designed to be a service for friends, family and co-workers to communicate and stay connected through exchange of quick and frequent updates

**The United States
and the Russian
Federation possess
roughly 90% of the
existing nuclear
weapons arsenal.**

to one simple question: what are you doing? It has instead emerged as a powerful communication tool for social causes and businesses.

All messages posted on the Twitter website must be 140 characters or less. This amount was chosen to match the limit for mobile phone text messages. It is sometimes difficult to fit a thought into just 140 characters, but this makes you really think about what you want to say, and to say it concisely. Twitter works by first creating a free account at **www.twitter. com** which gives you your own page to post updates. Anyone with a Twitter account can choose to "follow you"—that is, to read your updates.

An important part of tweeting is to get your followers to send something you post to all of their followers. This is called "re-tweeting". There is a multiplier effect built into the Twitter structure that makes it easier to reach a lot of people in a short time.

**TRANSLATION:** Communicating across languages can be made easier via free online translation services. You simply type into a box and choose the language to translate the document into. While these services are far from perfect, they offer a basic form of translation that can be useful for global youth activists to communicate with one another. Two popular services are **Yahoo! Babel Fish (www. babelfish.com)** and **Google Translate (translate.google.com)**.

# WRAPPING IT UP
# WITH GRATITUDE!

The primary purpose of *Action for Disarmament: 10 Things You Can Do* is to help you express yourself creatively as an agent for social change. Expressing ourselves is important and when we start with gratitude as an expression we can become more at ease in group situations (such as facilitating a meeting or giving a speech) and we can also quiet our minds when working alone (such as preparing for a presentation or writing a letter). Starting with gratitude means to think of those things in our lives that we are grateful for. Many things can be identified as "gratitude" like our homes or clean air to breathe, or the people we love or our favorite food or special place to visit. Research into happiness has shown that when we say "thank you" or feel grateful for what we have, that feeling increases our own sense of well-being. Moreover, when I say "thank you" to someone else, not only does it make me feel happy, but the person I am thanking feels happy too.

One way to practice expressing gratitude is to start a journal where you can keep track of what it is that you are grateful for. Everyday there are things that happen where we can find gratitude. Writing these and other things in a journal can help remind us of our own happiness and gratitude, which can help when things are not going well, or when we feel sad. It is often rewarding to look back on what we have written and remember what it is or was that caused us to be grateful.

Try this—Free write about three things you appreciate in your immediate surroundings. Then extend the circle of appreciation to three things you appreciate in your family and friends. Extending the circle ever outwards, write about three things you appreciate in your community, and extend that further to write about three things you appreciate in our world. Finally, write three things you appreciate about yourself, the person you are and the person you are becoming. If you want to, share this exercise with a friend. You will probably find reasons to be grateful!

 **TIP**

**If you create a website or use social media to create a campaign, consider tracking the success of your campaign by using Web Analytics tools like Google Analytics or social analytics tools for tracking sites like Facebook and Twitter. These provide information on who is using your sites. This data helps you evaluate whether you are succeeding in reaching your audience.**

"Railing against the past will not heal us. History has happened. It's over and done with. All we can do is to change its course by encouraging what we love instead of destroying what we don't. There is beauty yet in this brutal, damaged world of ours. Hidden, fierce, immense. Beauty that is uniquely ours and beauty that we have received with grace from others, enhanced, re-invented and made our own. We have to seek it out, nurture it, love it. Making bombs will only destroy us. It doesn't matter whether we use them or not. They will destroy us either way. I don't mean to be facetious, merely to point out that this is surely the short cut to hell. Nuclear weapons signify dreadful things. The end of imagination."

*Arundhati Roy, author and activist* ◀

# CONCLUSION

## UNITED NATIONS SECRETARY GENERAL'S CALL TO NUCLEAR DISARMAMENT

There are certainly more than Ten Things we can do for disarmament and non-proliferation. This work is not only for young people, but for all people. The UN Secretary-General, Ban Ki-moon has a five-point proposal that he calls "My Plan to Drop the Bomb". He wants disarmament to be verifiable, legally binding and re-invigorated by action through the UN Security Council. He is calling on countries to complete the ratification process for the Comprehensive Nuclear-Test-Ban Treaty so that the CTBT can enter into force. The Secretary-General has also emphasized the importance of transparency and accountability in order that those countries with nuclear weapons come clean about the size and location of their arsenals, and finally, that all weapons of mass destruction and their delivery systems be destroyed, including limiting missiles and conventional weapons so that other non-nuclear forces do not take away the real peace dividend that disarmament affords.

In an effort to *drop the bomb*, we might not only think about ridding the world of nuclear weapons and ending the illegal trafficking of small arms, *we should also aim to drop war altogether.* According to Article 26 of the UN Charter, we should establish "international peace and security with the least diversion for armaments of the world's human and economic resources". This is a step in the right direction. However, as we realize that no nation can solve today's threats to peace and security on its own, we will come to understand that war is ineffective and peace is not only possible but necessary. We are at a critical crossroads between reducing nuclear arsenals and seeing them proliferate. Similarly, timing is crucial to end the illicit movement of small arms which fuel conflict and insecurity around the globe. After years of stagnation, momentum is building to disarm now. There has never been a better time to get involved!

Sadako's statue in Hiroshima: Sadako Sasaki (7 January 1943-25 October 1955) was a Japanese girl who was two years old when the atomic bomb was dropped on 6 August 1945, near her home in Hiroshima, Japan. Sadako is remembered through the story of a thousand origami cranes before her death, and is to this day a symbol of innocent victims of war. Students continue to make these origami cranes in memory of her.

# UN CHARTER: ARTICLE 26

"In order to promote the establishment and maintenance of international peace and security with the least diversion for armaments of the world's human and economic resources, the Security Council shall be responsible for [...] the establishment of a system for the regulation of armaments."

# NOTE TO

In August 2002, the United Nations published a report on disarmament and non-proliferation (DNP) education. In the foreword, former Secretary-General Kofi Annan touched upon an important truth when he wrote that an entire generation was growing up without having known the terror of living under the threat of a global nuclear disaster. Disarmament education plays an important role in helping us to remember that this threat still exists. That remembering can be used as a powerful tool to build a clear understanding of the concepts and issues on how best to achieve international peace and security. The goal of *Action for Disarmament: 10 Things You Can Do* is to provide resources to help empower young people to participate in making decisions "both public and private" about disarmament and non-proliferation, and to hopefully increase their safety and security and ultimately the security of all humanity.

Disarmament education has changed a few times over the last decades. While the initial focus during the Cold War was on nuclear weapons, the geopolitical changes that took place in the 1990s opened the doors of multilateral disarmament to include the conventional arms trade, in particular small arms, light weapons and landmines. Today, DNP education has expanded to include the threat of terrorism. In particular, nuclear smuggling has become a source of concern. With the proliferation of nuclear technology, the potential for nuclear materials to be stolen or diverted has increased. Since 1993 there have been a number of confirmed cases of nuclear smuggling involving radioactive materials that could be used to make a radiological weapon. New threats demand new thinking. DNP education has the potential to play a critical role in engaging public participation to develop new strategies to reduce this threat.

Too often, information about conflict and the proliferation of weapons is retrospective, meaning the violence has already happened. Disarmament education asks: what can we do in the future to bring about a culture of peace, security, and

# EDUCATORS

human rights? We encourage you to approach this book in a proactive manner, and to use the various strategies for disarmament and non-proliferation in the future tense, to bring about change and transformation. Youth action is critical in this future tense, and empowering young people to become teachers and learners themselves is one of the goals of this book. Education for disarmament breaks with the entrenched passivity of learning and waiting for teachers to tell students what to do. This book is more a user manual of how young people can take action themselves to create change in the world. We encourage you to use any part of the book and to select the strategies that best fit your situation and concerns. These ideas are meant to help us all imagine a more peaceful world for the future, and make it happen in the present.

## THE UN EXPERT GROUP ON DISARMAMENT AND NON-PROLIFERATION EDUCATION

A teacher warns children about the threats of landmines and unexploded ordnance.

The UN Expert Group on Disarmament and Non-Proliferation Education was convened in accordance with General Assembly resolution 55/33 E to outline the future direction of DNP education. The six-point mandate of the Study produced by the UN Expert Group encouraged defining new methods for DNP education, and making recommendations for the implementation of this education at all levels of society. It encourages not only education about disarmament, but education for disarmament.

DNP education, as defined by the study, is concerned with the development of skills and knowledge to empower people to contribute to the process of disarmament, particularly nuclear

NOTE TO EDUCATORS

▲

143

Children wave the
United Nations flag.

weapons but also about better control of illicit small arms. DNP seeks to enhance both national and international security, by promoting the reduction of armaments to mutually agreed levels under effective controls, and by making connections between peace, security, and sustainable development. The study outlines several useful pedagogical ideas for DNP education, which recognize that each student is a resource of information, experiences, regional perspectives and insights. The pedagogy of DNP education prefers interactive learning techniques that support students' inquiries into disarmament and non-proliferation issues. These participatory strategies include: inquiry-based research to deepen knowledge, problem solving, small group discussions, critical listening, an appreciation of the complexity of issues and diversity of perspectives, clarification and reframing to create shared knowledge, and extension of learning and the application of understandings to different circumstances. This book aims to contribute to the emergence of critical consciousness and the development of skills and capacities to create social change.

# THREATS TO SECURITY

The idea that armed violence and war should be prevented or at least controlled is enshrined into the very essence of the UN Charter. The Preamble states that future generations should be saved from the scourge of war. The system of collective security that the UN founders adopted focused exclusively on military threats to security. Today, peace and security are no longer viewed in terms of the absence of military conflict alone. The common security interests of all people are also seen to be affected by poverty, hunger, environmental degradation and human rights violations, which are often at the heart of national and international tensions. The collective search for global stability is grounded in the complex interactions between security, development and human rights. They are inseparable.

International security is complex and many creative strategies are often needed at the same time to resolve conflicts and achieve peace. There are numerous reasons to advocate for disarmament and non-proliferation but the most important issue is the preservation of life—the life of individual human beings and the natural environment that sustains us all.

# PREAMBLE TO THE CHARTER OF THE UNITED NATIONS

## WE THE PEOPLES OF THE UNITED NATIONS DETERMINED

- to save succeeding generations from the scourge of war, which twice in our lifetime has brought untold sorrow to mankind, and

- to reaffirm faith in fundamental human rights, in the dignity and worth of the human person, in the equal rights of men and women and of nations large and small, and

- to establish conditions under which justice and respect for the obligations arising from treaties and other sources of international law can be maintained, and

- to promote social progress and better standards of life in larger freedom,

## AND FOR THESE ENDS

- to practice tolerance and live together in peace with one another as good neighbours, and

- to unite our strength to maintain international peace and security, and to ensure, by the acceptance of principles and the institution of methods, that armed force shall not be used, save in the common interest, and

- to employ international machinery for the promotion of the economic and social advancement of all peoples

- have resolved to combine our efforts to accomplish these aims.

Weapons and ammunition lie on the ground at a demobilization centre in the town of Bunia in the eastern region of Ituri, Democratic Republic of the Congo (DRC).

# PHOTO CREDITS

pg.4-5 © UNSMIL/Iason Foounten

pg.8 © National Archives

pg.9 © National Archives

pg.10 © Shigenobu Tsukiji

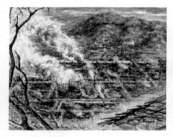
pg.10 © Kazuo Kawaguchi

pg.10 © Hiroko Yoshiyama

pg.13 © UNICEF/NYHQ2011-2415/
Jan Grarup

pg.17 © UN Photo/Martine Perret

pg.19 © UN Photo/Victoria Hazou

pg.21 © National Archives

pg.22 © UN Photo/Tobin Jones

pg.23 © UN Photo/Ky Chung

pg.24 © UN Photo/Tobin Jones

pg.28-29 © UNICEF/NYHQ2011-1980/Roger Lemoyne

pg.33 © UN Photo/Rick Bajornas

pg.37 © National Archives

pg.39 © Kazuo Kawaguchi

pg.40 © Shiego Hayashi

pg.41 © Hidetsugu Aihara

pg.43 © UN Photo/Mark Garten

pg.44-45 © UNICEF/INDA2011-00314/Niklas Halle'n

pg.49 © UN Photo/Paulo Filgueiras

pg.52-53 © UNICEF/NYHQ2004-1150/Giacomo Pirozzi

pg.57 © UNMAS/S. Carmichael

pg.58 © UNMAS Palestine

pg.63 © UNICEF/INDA2011-00208/
Niklas Halle'n

pg.64-65 © UN Photo/Martine Perret

pg.69 © REUTERS/Danish Siddiqui

pg.70 © UN Photo/Mark Garten

pg.73 © UN Photo/Tobin Jones

pg.75 © UNICEF/NYHQ2002-0440/
Giacomo Pirozzi

pg.76-77 © UNICEF/NYHQ2007-
2869/Giacomo Pirozzi

pg.81 © UNICEF/NYHQ2010-2852/
Brent Stirton

pg.82 © Viva Rio

pg.83 © UNICEF/NYHQ2007-2693/
Giacomo Pirozzi

pg.88-89 © UNICEF/BANA2013-
00314/Habibul Haque